Demonology

An Exciting Guide to Demons and Dark Creatures in World Mythology and Religions

Oscar Larsen

© **Copyright 2024 - All rights reserved.**

No part of this publication may be reproduced, distributed, or transmitted in any form or by any means, including photocopying, recording, or other electronic or mechanical methods, without the prior written permission of the publisher, except as permitted by U.S. copyright law.

Disclaimer Notice:

This publication is intended to provide accurate and authoritative information on the subject matter covered. While every effort has been made by the publisher and author to prepare this book, they make no representations or warranties as to the accuracy or completeness of the contents of this book and specifically disclaim any implied warranties of merchantability or fitness for a particular purpose. No warranties of any kind may be created or extended by sales representatives or written sales materials.

Table of Contents

ORIGINS — 5

ANCIENT MESOPOTAMIAN DEMONS — 7

DEMONIC FIGURES IN HINDU MYTHOLOGY — 19

BIBLICAL DEMONS AND ANGELS — 33

DEMONS IN ISLAMIC TEXTS — 48

DARK CREATURES OF JAPANESE FOLKLORE — 60

NORSE MYTHOLOGY'S DARK BEINGS — 72

DARK CREATURES IN SLAVIC MYTHOLOGY — 84

SPIRITS AND DEMONS IN AFRICAN FOLKLORE — 97

DEMONIC FIGURES OF CHINESE MYTHOLOGY — 111

MALEVOLENT ENTITIES OF NATIVE AMERICAN MYTHOLOGY — 122

AFTERWORD — 134

Origins

Historically, dark creatures have been integral to the narratives that form the backbone of cultures around the world. They often embody the antithesis of societal values and norms, representing chaos, evil, or destruction. This portrayal, however, is simplistic and overlooks the nuanced roles these beings play. In many traditions, dark creatures prompt introspection and moral evaluation by presenting challenges to gods and humans alike. Their interactions often lead to tales of caution, lessons of bravery, and the virtues of redemption.

From a theological perspective, these creatures stimulate the exploration of existential and metaphysical questions: Why does evil exist? What is the nature of suffering? How do we reconcile the presence of malevolence with the concept of a benevolent divine power? By examining these figures, we engage with fundamental aspects of human inquiry about the universe and our place within it.

Moreover, the study of these dark beings reveals much about the human psyche. They often personify internal fears, hidden desires, and the darker sides of human nature that many prefer to suppress or ignore. By bringing these elements to light through myth and religious narrative, societies can confront and negotiate the complexities of human emotion and morality.

This book seeks to uncover these layers of meaning, offering readers a comprehensive understanding of how dark mythical creatures are not just remnants of ancient fears but are vibrant elements of cultural heritage that continue to influence modern perceptions of the world. Through this exploration, we aim to provide a broader appreciation of these beings in a context that transcends their traditional roles as mere antagonists in mythic stories.

Ancient Mesopotamian Demons

The Mesopotamian pantheon, one of the earliest and most complex deistic systems in recorded history, is composed of a vast array of gods, goddesses, and supernatural beings. Central to Mesopotamian religion, these deities were deeply woven into the fabric of everyday life, governing all aspects of the natural and supernatural world. Among these entities were several demonic creatures, each with distinct roles and attributes, reflecting the Mesopotamians' nuanced understanding of good, evil, and the in-between.

Demonic entities in Mesopotamian mythology often served dual functions: they could be malevolent, bringing disease, famine, and misfortune, or they could fulfill protective roles, warding off evil and chaos. These beings were not strictly evil but were considered part of the natural order, necessary for maintaining balance and harmony in the universe.

Pazuzu

This figure is notably complex, intertwining aspects of fear, protection, and royal symbolism within the Mesopotamian religious context. Pazuzu is primarily known through Assyrian and Babylonian mythology, cultures renowned for their detailed record-keeping in cuneiform on clay tablets. He is often depicted as a fearsome creature, combining human and animal elements: a humanoid body, a scorpion's tail, two pairs of wings, the paws of a lion, and a serpentine penis. His face is typically that of a lion or dog, with an expression frozen in a menacing roar. This grotesque appearance was believed to ward off evil spirits and was particularly linked to banishing the malevolent goddess Lamashtu who preyed on pregnant women and infants.

Lamashtu's demonic activities included killing crops and livestock as well as causing harm to unborn and newborn babies. As a counter to these threats, Pazuzu's image was used in amulets and statues to protect those most vulnerable. Interestingly, while Pazuzu himself was feared, he was also considered a protector, embodying a dual nature that reflects the ambiguity of divine and demonic figures in Mesopotamian beliefs. This dual nature shows how the Mesopotamians understood the world in terms of balance and counterbalance, a theme prevalent in many ancient religions.

The use of Pazuzu's figure extends beyond mere protection. His image was not only found in households but also buried with the dead, and used in health-related rituals, indicating his important role in everyday life and the afterlife beliefs of the Mesopotamians. The invocation of Pazuzu could be seen as a form of sympathetic magic, where invoking the powerful and fearsome could protect against the threats of chaos and evil.

Moreover, Pazuzu's prominence can be linked to the royal symbolism and the broader protective strategies of the Assyrian empire. Kings of Assyria were often depicted as warrior-defenders of their people, battling chaos and disorder, roles paralleled in the protective aspects of Pazuzu. Thus, his image might also have been a reflection of the state's ideology, projecting power and protection under the aegis of the ruling class.

Theological perspectives on Pazuzu during the Assyrian and Babylonian periods were complex. The demon was not worshiped as a god but was invoked for his power to avert evil. This reflects a broader characteristic of Mesopotamian religious practice, which frequently blended magic with religion. Ritual practitioners such as exorcists and diviners held significant roles in this society, mediating the supernatural forces that affected everyday life. They would use figures like Pazuzu in rituals to cure ailments believed to be caused by supernatural entities, illustrating the practical and intertwined nature of religion and healthcare in ancient Mesopotamia.

In contemporary culture, Pazuzu has been portrayed variously in popular media, most famously in the 1973 film "The Exorcist," where he is erroneously identified as the possessing demon. Such portrayals, while diverging significantly from the original mythology, reflect the lasting impact of Mesopotamian culture on modern narratives and highlight how ancient myths and deities continue to influence contemporary culture in various, sometimes unexpected, ways.

Lamashtu

Described in ancient texts and depicted in artifacts, Lamashtu was no ordinary demon; she was a daughter of the sky god Anu, the supreme deity of the Mesopotamian pantheon. Her divine lineage, however, did not curb her malevolence. Instead, it endowed her with formidable powers, making her a feared figure among those who revered the pantheon of gods and goddesses for protection and prosperity.

Lamashtu's physical depiction in Mesopotamian art is both distinct and disturbing. She is often shown with a hairy body, a lioness' head with donkey's teeth and ears, long fingers and fingernails, and the feet of a bird with sharp talons. These features symbolize her predatory nature, aligning her with the wild and uncontrollable aspects of the natural world. She is typically depicted nursing a dog and a pig at her breasts, a stark contrast to the nurturing human mother figure, thus reinforcing her role as an antithetical force to maternal well-being.

The primary mythological narrative surrounding Lamashtu centers on her insatiable desire to harm mothers and their children. She was believed to prey upon women during childbirth, kidnap infants, suck their blood, and chew on their bones. Such graphic depictions of her actions were not merely for storytelling; they served as a serious warning to the dangers pregnant women and infants faced, highlighting the vulnerabilities at these critical stages of life.

In response to the threat posed by Lamashtu, ancient Mesopotamians sought protection through a variety of means. Amulets, spells, and rituals were commonly used to ward off her presence. These protective measures were deeply embedded in the Mesopotamian medical and magical practices, illustrating the blend of healthcare and spiritual protection that characterized their approach to dealing with supernatural threats.

One of the key figures involved in counteracting Lamashtu's wrath was Pazuzu, another demon, albeit with a protective aspect against her specific malice. Ironically, it was believed that only a demon could effectively combat another demon. Pazuzu's amulets and figurines, often depicted with him facing forward with a menacing expression, were used as talismans to protect against Lamashtu, demonstrating the complex interplay of fear and protection within the pantheon of Mesopotamian supernatural beings.

The rituals to exorcise Lamashtu also provide insight into the spiritual and religious life of ancient Mesopotamia. These rituals often involved elaborate ceremonies, including incantations and the use of symbolic objects that represented good health and divine protection. The priests and exorcists who performed these rites played a crucial role in the community, acting as intermediaries between the human and divine realms. Their ability to wield spiritual power underscored the societal belief in the tangible efficacy of religious rituals.

Moreover, Lamashtu's presence in Mesopotamian mythology has broader implications for understanding ancient views on gender and the role of women. Her depiction as a perverse maternal figure not only highlights deep-seated fears around motherhood and fertility but also reflects the anxieties about the destructive potential of female power in a predominantly patriarchal society. This aspect of her mythology opens a lens to the gender dynamics at play in ancient Mesopotamian culture, revealing the complex ways in which gender and power were conceptualized.

Gallu

The gallû demons are often associated with the netherworld, the dark and chaotic realm of the dead, where they execute various malevolent tasks. In cuneiform texts, which are among the most important sources for understanding Mesopotamian culture and religion, gallûs are depicted as terrifying forces. They are known for their ability to bring about sickness, possess individuals, and haunt desolate places. Their name, which can be translated to mean something akin to "great burner" or "devourer," reflects their feared abilities to consume and destroy.

Physically, gallû demons are not described in as much detail as some other Mesopotamian demons. What survives in art and text often portrays them as monstrous beings, sometimes with features that are a blend of human and animal elements—an attribute common in Mesopotamian demonic depictions. These features likely symbolized their liminal status, straddling the boundaries between the known world and the mysterious realm of the dead.

The role of gallû demons in mythology is often linked to their function in the underworld. They are frequently cited as servants or minions of major deities like Ereshkigal, the queen of the underworld, and Nergal, the god of death and plague. Their tasks included dragging unfortunate souls into the depths of the underworld, punishing lawbreakers, and enforcing divine justice. This aspect of their role highlights a common theme in Mesopotamian religious thought: the maintenance of order through divine and semi-divine agents who manage the cosmos's chaotic and destructive forces.

One of the most famous narratives involving a gallû demon is the Descent of Inanna, an epic myth where the goddess Inanna descends into the underworld. In this story, gallû demons play a critical role as the enforcers of the underworld's queen, Ereshkigal. They are dispatched to bring Inanna into the netherworld, highlighting their role as agents of a higher divine power and as crucial figures in the enactment of celestial and terrestrial decrees.

The fear of gallû demons was so profound that it permeated daily life and ritual practice in ancient Mesopotamia. Amulets, incantations, and exorcisms specifically designed to ward off gallûs were common, indicating the pervasive anxiety surrounding these demonic figures. These protective measures were not merely superstitious practices; they were deeply embedded within the medical and spiritual frameworks of the time. Healers and exorcists, often priests, employed complex rituals to protect individuals from the harm that gallûs could cause, reflecting an intricate understanding of health and illness that intertwined the physical with the spiritual.

Asag

Asag, a demon whose name evokes dread in the ancient Mesopotamian texts, represents one of the most formidable entities in the Sumerian demonic pantheon. Unlike the more protective or ambivalent demons like

Pazuzu or the maternal destroyer Lamashtu, Asag is consistently depicted as a malignant force associated with the elemental power of sickness and disease, particularly those affecting the earth and its fertility.

The mythological context of Asag places him as a demon who causes disease, not just in humans but in the land itself, blighting crops and making waters undrinkable. His very presence is said to turn the rivers to stone, a vivid metaphor for the devastating effect he could have on the natural environment and, by extension, on agricultural productivity and the well-being of entire communities. This depiction reflects the ancient Mesopotamians' deep connection with their environment and the significance they placed on the health of the land as foundational to their survival and prosperity.

In art and literature, Asag is seldom portrayed directly, but his influence is characterized by the desolation he brings. The lack of visual representations may be due to the abstract nature of his domain—disease and the decay of nature—elements that are challenging to personify in a concrete form. However, the descriptions of his actions in mythological texts are graphic and detailed, emphasizing his role as an adversary to the well-being of both land and people.

One of the primary myths where Asag features prominently is in his battle with the god Ninurta, a warrior deity and the god of farming among other roles. In this narrative, Asag assembles an army of rock demons, a symbolic cohort that further cements his connection with the destructive forces of nature. Ninurta's eventual victory over Asag is not just a triumph of a god over a demon but represents the reassertion of order and fertility over chaos and blight. This mythological motif, where a divine hero combats a monstrous adversary, is a common theme in many ancient cultures, encapsulating the eternal struggle between order and chaos, health and disease, fertility and barrenness.

The battle between Ninurta and Asag also highlights the role of divine intervention in maintaining the balance of the natural world, a concept that was central to Mesopotamian religious belief. The gods were seen as the ultimate guarantors of the cycle of the seasons and the fertility of the earth, which were critical for the survival of an agrarian society. Asag's defeat, therefore, is not merely a military triumph but a necessary act to restore the cosmic balance and ensure the land's productivity.

In addition to his mythological role, Asag's presence in the religious and cultural life of ancient Mesopotamia can be seen in the various incantations and rituals designed to ward off his influence. These texts often include elaborate spells and rituals invoking powerful gods to counteract the diseases and agricultural devastation that Asag could bring. Such practices reflect the ancient Mesopotamians' pragmatic approach to their gods and demons, seeking their favor not just in matters of spiritual or ethical significance but also in the very practical aspects of health and survival.

Asag's role as a demon of sickness links him to the broader Mesopotamian understanding of health and disease. Disease was often seen as a supernatural affliction rather than a natural phenomenon, and the role of demons like

Asag was integral in this perception. Healing rituals and medical treatments thus frequently took on a religious dimension, involving incantations and ceremonies intended to expel demonic forces from the body and from the land.

Rabisu

Rabisu, a demon from ancient Mesopotamian mythology, embodies the quintessential characteristics of an ambush predator, lurking at the threshold of spaces, ready to pounce on the unsuspecting. Translated from Akkadian, the name "Rabisu" carries the meaning of "the one who lies in wait," and this demon's reputation in the mythological lore of the ancient Near East is precisely that of a sinister presence poised to strike.

The Rabisu demon is often mentioned in ancient texts alongside other malevolent entities, but it holds a unique niche within this demonic hierarchy. Unlike the broader destructive forces represented by demons like Lamashtu or Pazuzu, Rabisu's threat is more direct and immediate, often associated with unexpected danger and the violation of boundaries. This demon's portrayal as a threshold guardian, or rather a threshold violator, reflects deep-seated cultural anxieties about the sanctity and safety of personal and communal spaces.

In iconography and literature, Rabisu is not often depicted in detail, which perhaps adds to the unsettling nature of this demon—the unseen is always more frightening. However, the descriptions available paint a picture of a demon that could assume both visible and invisible forms.

When visible, it is portrayed as a dark, menacing figure, often cloaked, which is symbolic of its association with secrecy and sudden, malicious intent. The invisibility of Rabisu speaks to its other attribute: the ability to hide in any nook or cranny, waiting for the moment to attack. This attribute made Rabisu particularly feared, as it could be anywhere and strike at any time without warning.

The cultural significance of Rabisu extends into the practical measures taken by ancient Mesopotamians to protect themselves from such demonic threats. Doorways, thresholds, and windows—being transitional spaces between the secure interior and the uncertain exterior—were considered vulnerable points through which a Rabisu might enter. To counter this threat, various amulets and inscriptions were placed in these areas. Incantations and rituals specifically designed to ward off Rabisu were common, involving the use of magical bowls, statues, or plaques that bore protective symbols or cuneiform inscriptions invoking the protection of more powerful gods.

These protective practices highlight an essential aspect of Mesopotamian life: the integration of magic and religion into daily routines. The Mesopotamians did not see a clear distinction between the supernatural and the natural world; both were interwoven into their understanding of reality. Thus, the steps taken to protect oneself from demonic forces like Rabisu were not merely superstitious acts but were supported by a structured system of beliefs and rituals that were as integral to daily life as practical tasks.

The fear of Rabisu can be seen as a reflection of broader societal concerns. In a world where death and misfortune could easily be attributed to unseen supernatural forces, Rabisu's characteristics as an ambush predator symbolized the ever-present danger of life's uncertainties. The rituals and symbols used to ward off such a demon were not only about protecting the physical space but also about asserting control over the unpredictable and often hostile forces that people felt were at play in the world around them.

Rabisu also plays into the ancient Mesopotamian views of morality and justice. The suddenness of Rabisu's attacks could be interpreted as a form of divine retribution for transgressions or as a test of one's vigilance and moral fortitude.

Demonic Figures in Hindu Mythology

Hinduism, with its rich myths and legends, hosts an extensive pantheon of deities and an array of spiritual beings that range from benevolent to malevolent. Within this broad spectrum, dark creatures play significant roles, serving as symbols of moral and cosmic dualities, and contributing to the religion's intricate narrative of dharma (duty, righteousness, and moral law) and adharma (that which is not in accordance with dharma).

Hinduism characterizes its spiritual beings within a structured hierarchy where gods and goddesses preside over various aspects of the universe and human life. Lesser deities, spirits, and creatures have specific roles, contributing to the moral and spiritual lessons taught through sacred texts and folklore.

Within this structure, dark creatures, often referred to as asuras (demons), rakshasas (man-eating beings), and other malevolent spirits, serve as antagonists in numerous stories and epics. These beings are typically portrayed as disrupting the cosmic order, challenging the gods, and tempting or terrorizing humans, thereby testing devotion and virtue.

Dark creatures in Hindu mythology often embody the challenges faced by individuals as they strive to live righteously. They are not merely obstacles but are integral to the understanding of dharma. By confronting these beings, heroes and gods in myths demonstrate moral lessons and the importance of virtue.

The stories involving these dark creatures are not just mythological entertainment but are part of religious teachings and cultural education. They are dramatized in festivals, theatrical performances, and literature, reinforcing moral values and the metaphysical concepts of Hinduism.

Theologically, the existence of dark creatures in Hinduism underscores the religion's view of the universe as a dynamic balance of good and evil forces, where both are necessary for the moral and spiritual evolution of the soul. This duality is essential for creating the conditions under which humans can exercise free will and grow through the challenges they face.

Kali: The Dark Goddess of Destruction and Renewal

Kali, one of Hinduism's most enigmatic and powerful deities, encapsulates the profound dualities of destruction and creation, fear and love, chaos and order. Often misunderstood by those outside the Hindu tradition, her iconography and myths reveal deep philosophical and theological insights into the nature of time, change, and morality. As a goddess, Kali embodies the fierce aspect of the divine feminine, challenging conventional perceptions of life, death, and spiritual liberation.

Kali's name derives from the Sanskrit root word 'kāla,' which means time, but also darkness, indicating her association with both the eternal forces of time and the transformative power of darkness. This connection frames Kali as a goddess who transcends the good-evil dichotomy, embodying the necessary force of destruction that precedes renewal. In artistic depictions, Kali is often portrayed with a dark or black complexion, symbolizing the void from which all life springs and into which it ultimately dissolves. She wears a garland of severed heads and a skirt of dismembered arms, symbolizing the cutting of attachments and egos, and holds weapons and a severed head, signifying the defeat of ignorance and illusion.

The most renowned myth involving Kali is her battle with the demon Raktabija. During this conflict, every drop of blood Raktabija shed gave birth to more demons as it touched the ground. Kali, in her boundless ferocity, thus spread her tongue over the battlefield, catching the drops of blood before they could spawn more demons, and eventually defeated all manifestations of the demon. This narrative highlights Kali's role as a destroyer of evil and as a powerful force of nature that maintains cosmic order. It also illustrates her willingness to confront and absorb the negativity and pollution of the world to protect the universe and restore balance.

Kali's ferocity is matched by her maternal affection. She is revered as a caring mother who is fiercely protective of her devotees. In many communities, she is worshipped as the ultimate reality or the highest form of God by her devotees who see her fearsome aspects as expressions of her compassion, as she liberates her children from ignorance and egoism in the most direct way possible. This duality of Kali's character as both terrifying and nurturing reveals the deep symbolism of her mythology, which embraces life's complexity, acknowledging that life involves destruction, fear, love, and renewal.

Kali's significance extends beyond the physical and metaphysical to encapsulate a broader spiritual message. She is often associated with cremation grounds, symbolizing places where the body dissolves and the soul is freed from the cycle of death and rebirth. These grounds, where the five elements (earth, water, fire, air, and space) commingle, represent the edge of the known world, the border between civilization and the wild, between life and death. Kali's presence in these liminal spaces underscores her role as a guide through transitions, particularly from life to death, reminding her followers of the impermanence of life and the illusion of bodily existence.

Moreover, Kali plays a crucial role in the Shakta tradition of Hinduism, where she is considered a powerful expression of Shakti, the divine feminine energy. She challenges societal norms and traditional roles assigned to women, representing a form of femininity that is autonomous, strong, and liberating. Her unapologetic power and independence make her an icon of empowerment for many, resonating with contemporary themes of feminism and social justice.

Kali's festivals, such as Kali Puja, which is prominently celebrated in Bengal, involve rituals that embrace her transformative power. These rituals often take place at night, the time most strongly associated with her. Devotees offer animal sacrifices, a controversial and often misunderstood practice that symbolizes the surrender of one's animal instincts and ego, and partake in songs, dances, and acts of devotion that express both the joy and solemnity of encountering the divine in its most raw form.

Kali is a multi-dimensional figure who commands awe and reverence as she encapsulates the cycle of life and death. Her worship challenges adherents to confront their fears, understand their impermanence, and seek the deeper spiritual truths of existence. Through the lens of Kali, we are invited to embrace the entirety of life's experiences, recognizing the divine play of creation and destruction that characterizes the cosmos and the human condition alike.

Rakshasas

Rakshasas occupy a prominent place in Hindu mythology, embodying the complex interplay of moral, spiritual, and cosmic forces. These beings are typically portrayed as demons or malevolent spirits with a penchant for disruption, deception, and destruction. However, the depiction of rakshasas is not uniformly negative, as these entities sometimes show a capacity for change, benevolence, or a role that serves a larger divine purpose. Understanding rakshasas offers a window into the broader themes of dharma (moral order), karma (action and consequence), and the ongoing struggle between good and evil that pervades Hindu religious narratives.

The origins of rakshasas are described in various Hindu scriptures, where they are often created by Brahma, the creator god, to be guardians or warriors. However, due to their aggressive and tumultuous nature, they are more frequently associated with the darker aspects of the cosmos. Physically, rakshasas are depicted as fearsome creatures, sometimes with the heads of animals like lions or elephants, and with large bodies, fierce eyes, and a terrifying presence. They possess the power to change their shapes, becoming invisible or altering their forms to deceive humans and gods alike.

Rakshasas are most famously referenced in Hindu epics like the Ramayana and the Mahabharata, where their interactions with gods and heroes shape much of the action and moral lessons of these stories. In the Ramayana, Ravana, the king of the rakshasas, abducts Sita, the wife of Rama, setting off a series of events that culminate in a grand battle and the eventual triumph of good over evil. Ravana, though a rakshasa, is also a complex character—a devout devotee of Shiva, a learned scholar, and a capable ruler, his character underscores the nuanced portrayal of rakshasas in Hindu mythology.

In the Mahabharata, other rakshasas appear with significant roles, both antagonistic and supportive. Ghatotkacha, the son of the Pandava Bhima and the rakshasi Hidimbi, fights on the side of the Pandavas during the great battle of Kurukshetra. His participation highlights the potential for rakshasas to integrate into the dharmic (righteous) framework of Hindu ethics, fighting for justice despite their demonic heritage.

The narrative roles of rakshasas extend beyond mere opposition to the heroes of Hindu mythology. They serve as catalysts for the unfolding of karmic and dharmic lessons that are central to the spiritual literature of India. The conflicts involving rakshasas often bring about situations where moral and spiritual dilemmas are presented, tested, and resolved, thereby allowing human and divine characters alike to evolve and fulfill their destinies.

Culturally, rakshasas are also significant in various Hindu festivals and rituals, particularly during occasions like Dussehra and Diwali, which celebrate the victory of good over evil, light over darkness, and knowledge over ignorance. The defeat of Ravana by Rama during Dussehra is a symbolic reaffirmation of these themes, deeply embedded in the cultural psyche and observed with performances of the Ramayana, effigy burnings, and dramatic reenactments.

In Hindu thought, rakshasas, like all beings, are subject to the laws of karma and dharma, and their actions have consequences that affect their spiritual evolution. This perspective allows for a more dynamic interpretation of what constitutes evil or adversarial forces, viewing them as integral to the cosmic and moral balance.

In modern interpretations, the symbolism of rakshasas resonates in discussions about human nature, ethics, and the internal and external battles individuals face. Their stories are relevant in exploring themes of power, responsibility, redemption, and the transformational potential of adhering to or deviating from dharma.

Vetala

Vetala occupies a unique niche in the vast expanse of Indian folklore and religious narratives. These spirits, akin to ghosts or revenants in Western mythology, are most famously chronicled in the ancient collection of tales known as the "Vetala Panchavimshati" or "Baital Pachisi." These stories encapsulate the complex interplay of ethics, duty, and metaphysical puzzles, presenting Vetala as both a disruptor and a teacher who challenges the living with riddles that probe the mysteries of life and death.

Vetalas are described as spirits that inhabit and animate dead bodies, preventing them from decaying, and thus lingering between life and death. Unlike ghosts, which are typically considered to be mere spirits of the deceased, vetalas are thought to possess corpses and use them for mobility, giving them a physical yet eerie presence. This liminality makes vetalas particularly fascinating subjects within Hindu mythology as they embody the transition from life to death, existing in a state that is neither fully alive nor entirely dead.

The primary source of vetala lore is found in the aforementioned "Vetala Panchavimshati." In this collection, a king named Vikramaditya is tasked with capturing a vetala that hangs from a tree in a cremation ground, embodying the vetala's connection to death and the macabre. Each time Vikramaditya captures the vetala and tries to carry it away, the vetala tells him a story that ends with a moral dilemma presented in the form of a question. If the king knows the answer and responds, the vetala returns to the tree, forcing the king to begin his task anew. If the king remains silent, the vetala promises to stay captured. However, the tales are so compelling that Vikramaditya feels compelled to respond. This narrative device not only highlights the vetala's supernatural cunning but also serves as a medium for discussing ethical and philosophical questions.

The figure of the vetala becomes a vehicle for imparting wisdom and moral guidance. The stories posed by the vetala challenge Vikramaditya—and by extension, the listener or reader—to consider complex issues of morality, justice, duty, and sacrifice. The dilemmas often have no clear right or wrong answers, reflecting the complexities of life's ethical decisions. This literary method of engaging with philosophical questions through narrative is a hallmark of many ancient cultures, and in the case of the vetala tales, it serves to engage issues of dharma (righteousness or duty) within the Hindu philosophical framework.

Vetalas are often associated with protection as well as malevolence. In some regions, they are considered guardian spirits, akin to the Western concept of gargoyles, which protect temples and villages from more malevolent forces. This protective aspect contrasts with their more unsettling, eerie portrayal and highlights the dual nature of many mythological beings, which can be both benevolent and dangerous depending on the context.

The lore of vetalas also touches on themes of death and the afterlife, integral elements of Hindu cosmology. The cremation grounds where vetalas are said to reside are places of powerful transformation—where the body is returned to the elements and the soul is believed to be released from the cycle of death and rebirth. The vetala's presence in such locations underscores their role as mediators between the material and spiritual worlds, navigating the boundaries of life and death.

In modern interpretations, vetalas continue to capture the imagination in various forms of media, from literature to television. They are often reimagined in contemporary horror or fantasy genres, reflecting universal fascinations with the undead and the supernatural. However, their traditional portrayals in Hindu literature offer a more nuanced view, presenting them not merely as creatures of horror but as complex entities that challenge the living to ponder deeper existential and moral questions.

Ravana

Ravana, the legendary king of Lanka, is a pivotal figure in Hindu mythology, most famously depicted as the primary antagonist in the ancient Indian epic, the Ramayana. His character is a complex amalgamation of brilliance and brutality, embodying both the heights of royal and scholarly achievement and the depths of demonic malevolence.

Born to a sage father, Vishrava, and a demoness mother, Kaikesi, Ravana was of the Brahmin caste through his father's lineage and a Rakshasa through his mother's. This dual heritage endowed him with a mix of Brahmanical intellect and demonic ferocity, making him a unique and formidable character. He performed severe penances and austerities to please Lord Shiva, from whom he obtained powerful celestial weapons and boons that made him nearly invincible. Ravana's devotion to Shiva also granted him profound knowledge and mastery over the Vedas and the arts, positioning him as one of the most learned characters in Hindu lore.

However, Ravana's narrative is predominantly marked by his abduction of Sita, the wife of Rama, which sets the stage for the main events of the Ramayana. This act, often interpreted as a consequence of his hubris and lust, ultimately leads to his downfall, fulfilling a curse pronounced upon him earlier for his misdeeds. It is this act that paints Ravana not just as a mere antagonist but as a tragic figure, whose virtues are overshadowed by his vices.

Ravana's kingdom, Lanka, is described as a place of magnificent beauty and wealth, a city of gold. Under his rule, it was a well-protected fortress, prosperous and advanced in technology and infrastructure. His rule, albeit marred by his tyrannical tendencies, was also marked by considerable administrative efficiency and patronage of the arts, suggesting that Ravana was not merely a tyrant but a capable and sometimes benevolent ruler.

The complexity of Ravana's character is further enhanced by his familial relationships and his role as a king, brother, and devotee. His fierce love and loyalty towards his family, particularly his devotion to his brother Kumbhakarna and his sister Shurpanakha, show a more personal and relatable side to him, contrasting sharply with his fearsome prowess and ruthless ambitions. These relationships humanize Ravana, offering a glimpse into his personal trials and the motivations behind his actions.

In the context of Hindu philosophy, Ravana exemplifies the perpetual conflict between good and evil, and the consequences of adharma (unrighteous actions). His story serves as a cautionary tale about the dangers of letting power, pride, and passion override wisdom and moral judgment. Despite his knowledge and capabilities, Ravana's failure to uphold dharma ultimately leads to his demise, emphasizing the moral of the Ramayana: that righteousness, no matter how challenged, ultimately prevails.

Ravana's defeat by Rama, an avatar of Lord Vishnu, is not just a physical conquest but a spiritual restoration of dharma. This battle is celebrated annually on the festival of Dussehra, symbolizing the victory of good over evil, light over darkness, and knowledge over ignorance. The effigy of Ravana is burned, and his story is retold, reminding people of the fine balance between virtue and vice, and the enduring power of righteousness.

Narakasura

Narakasura, also known as Naraka, is a significant figure in Hindu mythology, particularly within the narratives associated with the festival of Diwali. His story is predominantly recounted in the Puranic texts, which are a genre of important Hindu religious scriptures. Narakasura's tale highlights themes of tyranny, redemption, and the triumph of good over evil, encapsulating deep moral and ethical lessons that resonate within the broader cultural and religious practices of Hinduism.

Narakasura was the son of Bhudevi (the Earth goddess) and Varaha, an avatar of Lord Vishnu. This divine and royal lineage endowed him with remarkable powers and virtues. Initially, Naraka was a benevolent ruler and protector of his kingdom, Pragjyotisha, which was fortified with magical mountains and guarded by mystical beings. However, as time passed, he succumbed to arrogance and the corrupting influence of power, transforming into a tyrant feared by gods and humans alike.

According to the legends, Narakasura's tyranny reached its zenith when he stole the earrings of Aditi, the mother of gods, and abducted 16,000 daughters of the gods and sages, imprisoning them in his palace. This act of defiance and cruelty alarmed the heavens, leading to his eventual downfall. The gods appealed to Lord Krishna, an avatar of Vishnu, to defeat the demon king and restore dharma (cosmic law and order).

The battle between Krishna and Narakasura is a dramatic and pivotal episode. Krishna, accompanied by his wife Satyabhama—who is considered an incarnation of Bhudevi, Naraka's mother—attacked the fortress of Pragjyotisha. After a fierce combat, during which Krishna cleverly involved Satyabhama in the fight, Narakasura was killed by Satyabhama, fulfilling a prophecy that he would meet his end at the hands of his mother. This narrative twist not only highlights the poetic justice typical of Hindu mythology but also underscores the role of divine femininity in the restoration of balance.

The death of Narakasura is celebrated as Naraka Chaturdashi, a major part of the Diwali festival, symbolizing the destruction of evil and the light of wisdom dispelling the darkness of ignorance. In regions like West Bengal and the eastern states of India, this celebration is marked by lighting fireworks and lamps, illustrating the victory of light over darkness.

The liberation of the 16,000 women by Krishna also carries significant symbolic weight. Instead of returning to their homes, where they would likely have been stigmatized due to their long captivity, these women were respectfully integrated into Krishna's household, an act that not only restored their dignity but also challenged prevailing norms around honor and purity. This aspect of the story promotes themes of forgiveness, societal duty, and the reformation of individuals and society.

Narakasura's narrative is often interpreted as an allegory for the inner battles that individuals face against their lower instincts and ego. Narakasura, a being with divine origins, represents the potential for both greatness and fallibility within everyone. His eventual defeat symbolizes the need for ethical conduct and the importance of adhering to one's righteous duties, irrespective of one's power or position.

Biblical Demons and Angels

The Bible makes distinctions between demons and fallen angels, although the lines can sometimes blur due to variations in interpretations and translations. Generally, fallen angels are those celestial beings who rebelled against God and were cast out of heaven, while demons are often understood as evil spirits that may torment or possess individuals.

The most notable of the fallen angels is Lucifer, also known as Satan, who is depicted as having been an archangel of great beauty and power. Demons in the Bible are often depicted as unclean or evil spirits who may possess individuals and cause physical or mental illness. The Gospels, particularly the Synoptic Gospels (Matthew, Mark, and Luke), contain numerous accounts of Jesus casting out demons, indicating their recognition as malignant forces at odds with divine will.

Lucifer: The Fall from Grace and Transformation into Satan

Lucifer, often conflated with the figure of Satan or the Devil in Christian tradition, possesses a complex narrative history that intertwines with theology, literature, and cultural perception. The name "Lucifer," meaning "light-bringer" or "morning star," originates from the Latin word 'lucifer', which was used in the Vulgate, the Latin translation of the Bible, to translate the Hebrew word 'helel' (shining one). This term appears in Isaiah 14:12, where it describes a fallen Babylonian king, lamenting his pride and fall from power. Over time, this passage has been interpreted by some to symbolize the fall of Satan, and thus, the name Lucifer became associated with the devil, particularly in Christian tradition.

In this key biblical text, the imagery of a fallen morning star serves as a metaphor for pride and downfall, themes central to the Christian understanding of Lucifer. The passage reads, "How you are fallen from heaven, O Day Star, son of Dawn! How you are cut down to the ground, you who laid the nations low!" Initially, this was not directly linked to Satan; however, by the post-New Testament era, interpretations began to change. Early Christian writers, like Origen and St. Jerome, contributed to the evolving story of a celestial being who rebelled against God and was cast down as a result.

This transformation is deeply embedded in the broader Christian narrative of sin and redemption. According to traditional Christian doctrine, Lucifer was created as a powerful and beautiful angel, possibly one of the cherubim, who was endowed with significant authority and brilliance. However, his beauty and power fostered pride, leading him to aspire to ascend above his peers and equal God. This pride constituted his primary sin—hubris—which led to his rebellion and subsequent fall from grace. Thus, Lucifer became Satan, the adversary, opposing God and embodying evil and temptation.

The story of Lucifer's fall is often used to illustrate theological concepts such as the origin of evil, the nature of free will, and the consequences of pride. In Christian theology, Lucifer's rebellion is the first sin, preceding even the original sin of Adam and Eve, and serves as a profound allegory about the dangers and consequences of rebelling against divine order. His story emphasizes the Christian belief in the cosmic struggle between good and evil, with humanity caught in the middle, subject to Satan's temptations but also offered redemption through Christ.

Lucifer's narrative also permeates literary and cultural contexts, where his character has been variously interpreted. In John Milton's "Paradise Lost," Lucifer is portrayed with complexity, almost a tragic figure whose charisma and eloquence garner a degree of sympathy. Milton's Lucifer famously declares, "Better to reign in Hell than serve in Heaven," encapsulating his indomitable pride and rebellion. This portrayal has deeply influenced the modern cultural and literary depiction of Lucifer, often emphasizing his attributes of rebellion against tyranny, quest for independence, and tragic fall.

The figure of Lucifer has been adopted in various modern philosophical and cultural expressions as a symbol of enlightenment, individualism, and resistance against arbitrary authority. In some contemporary religious and spiritual movements, such as certain branches of Satanism, Lucifer is revered not as the devil but as a liberator or a source of knowledge, echoing the original meaning of his name as the light-bringer.

Lilith

Lilith, a figure shrouded in mystery and layered with cultural and theological interpretations, emerges from the annals of mythology not just as a mere demonic entity but as a symbol of rebellion, independence, and complexity. Her origins, while obscure and debated, are often linked to various ancient Near Eastern religions, and she gains significant prominence in Jewish folklore and mysticism.

The earliest references to a figure similar to Lilith are found in Sumerian texts, where she appears as Lilitu, a class of spirits associated with wind and storm and thought to be harmful to pregnant women and infants. These spirits are not clearly defined as a singular Lilith but share characteristics that prefigure the later Jewish interpretations.

Lilith's most famous mythological narrative comes from the Alphabet of Ben-Sira, an anonymous collection of Jewish texts from the Middle Ages. According to this narrative, Lilith was the first wife of Adam, created from the same earth as him to ensure equality. However, conflict arose when Lilith refused to become subservient to Adam. When her demands for equality were not met, she chose to leave Eden rather than compromise her autonomy. Calling upon God's name, she flew away to the Red Sea, a place associated with demons and other outcast spirits. In response, God sent three angels to bring her back, but she refused, choosing her independence over a return to Eden.

The angels then pronounced that one hundred of her children would die each day as punishment, establishing her role as a symbol of rebellion but also of loss and pain. In retaliation, Lilith was said to have power over newborn children, particularly male infants, whom she could endanger until their circumcision on the eighth day after birth, a belief that contributed to her demonization.

In the Jewish mystical tradition of Kabbalah, Lilith becomes even more complex. She is often associated with the Qliphoth, representations of evil or impure spiritual forces. Kabbalistic texts sometimes depict her as the consort of Samael (an archangel often associated with severity and death), and together, they embody a counter-divine force, challenging the harmonious structures of the Sephirot (the Tree of Life in Kabbalah).

Lilith's portrayal over centuries has often mirrored societal views on gender and sexuality. She is frequently depicted as a seductress or a witch, utilizing her sexuality as a form of power and a means of corruption. This characterization reflects deep-seated fears and taboos around female sexuality and agency, portraying Lilith as a figure who must be controlled or subdued.

However, in modern feminist interpretations, Lilith has been reclaimed as a symbol of female empowerment, resistance against patriarchal authority, and the struggle for equality. This contemporary view celebrates her decision to leave Eden as an act of courage and self-respect, turning Lilith from a demonized figure into a feminist icon.

The varying depictions of Lilith—from ancient demon to medieval seductress, to modern feminist symbol—highlight the fluidity of mythological characters and their adaptability to different cultural needs and social mores. Each interpretation offers insight into the period in which it was created, reflecting evolving attitudes towards gender, independence, and morality. In literature and art, Lilith has been a popular subject, portrayed in myriad ways that often emphasize her dual nature as both empowering and dangerous.

Asmodeus

Asmodeus, a figure steeped in ancient and medieval lore, appears across various cultural and religious traditions, each portraying him in a slightly different light. Most commonly recognized in Jewish and Christian demonology, Asmodeus embodies the archetype of lust and wrath, weaving a complex narrative thread through folklore, scripture, and mystical texts.

The name "Asmodeus" is derived from the Avestan language, where a similar name, Aeshma-daeva, appears in Zoroastrian texts. Aeshma is one of the daevas (demons) and is associated with wrath and anger. This connection suggests that Asmodeus's roots lie deep in the pre-Islamic lore of the Middle East, later assimilating into Jewish and Christian demonologies through cultural exchanges over centuries.

In Jewish tradition, Asmodeus is most famously detailed in the Book of Tobit, part of the Apocrypha. Here, Asmodeus falls in love with Sarah, the daughter of Raguel, and kills each of her seven husbands on their wedding night before the marriage can be consummated. This recurring tragedy is attributed to Asmodeus's jealousy and lust. Tobit's narrative is pivotal as it introduces Raphael, one of the archangels, who helps Tobias, the son of Tobit, to successfully marry Sarah and banish Asmodeus. The story not only showcases Asmodeus's malevolence but also reinforces themes of divine intervention and redemption.

The Talmud elaborates further on Asmodeus, providing insights into his abilities and characteristics. He is portrayed as a king of demons, a creature of fire, and a being of cunning intelligence, capable of rising through the celestial hierarchy to challenge Solomon, the wise king of Israel. According to lore, Asmodeus even temporarily displaces Solomon, stealing his identity and throne, thereby demonstrating his potent capabilities and threat to order and righteousness.

In these narratives, Asmodeus is not merely a symbol of individual sins such as lust or wrath but represents a profound existential threat, challenging divine and kingly authority. His interactions with Solomon are particularly telling, as they delve into themes of wisdom, power, and the vulnerability of even the wisest of rulers. This portion of Asmodeus's lore underscores the perpetual battle between good and evil, knowledge and deception, which permeates much of religious and moral teachings.

Christian demonology, particularly during the medieval period, further embellished Asmodeus's characteristics and domains. In this context, he becomes one of the princes of Hell, often associated specifically with the deadly sin of lust. Medieval grimoires, such as the Lesser Key of Solomon, categorize him as a powerful demon who must be summoned and controlled with caution. These texts often provide elaborate descriptions of rituals for invoking Asmodeus, reflecting the era's fascination with the occult and the complex hierarchies of hellish beings.

Moreover, Asmodeus's role in influencing human affairs, particularly through instigating sexual temptation, is emphasized in Christian demonology. He is frequently depicted overseeing brothels and encouraging licentious behavior, linking him directly to the moral decay of individuals and societies. This portrayal taps into deeper fears and warnings about the seductive power of evil and the vigilance required to maintain virtue.

Asmodeus appears in various literary works, which explore his demonic nature and interaction with humanity. One notable example is in the "Dictionnaire Infernal" by Collin de Plancy, a 19th-century compendium of demonology that illustrates Asmodeus and other demons, embedding them in the popular imagination as characters with distinct personalities and histories.

Beelzebub

Beelzebub, a figure whose name has become synonymous with demonic power and malevolence, has a complex history rooted in ancient texts and developed through medieval Christian demonology.

The name "Beelzebub" can be traced back to the Philistine god Baal-Zebub, which appears in the biblical text of 2 Kings. In this context, Baal-Zebub is referred to as the god of Ekron, one of the five cities of the Philistine pentapolis, and is translated as "Lord of the Flies." The etymology of

Baal-Zebub is a subject of scholarly debate, with interpretations ranging from a derisive reworking of "Baal-Zebul," meaning "Lord Prince," to a literal designation that could imply a deity associated with pestilence or protection against insects.

The transformation from Baal-Zebub to Beelzebub in a Judeo-Christian context represents more than a simple transliteration; it reflects a process of demonization whereby local deities of conquered or rival peoples were incorporated into the Hebrew religious framework as demonic figures. This practice was not only theological but also served as a form of cultural hegemony, delegitimizing and vilifying the gods of subjugated peoples.

In the New Testament, Beelzebub is explicitly linked with demonic activity. In the synoptic gospels, he is identified as the prince of demons, an adversary whom Jesus is accused of consorting with to perform exorcisms. The Pharisees accuse Jesus of casting out demons by the power of "Beelzebub, the prince of demons," to which Jesus responds with a discourse on the division within a kingdom being a path to its fall, thereby refuting the claim by highlighting the illogicality of Satan casting out Satan.

As Christianity spread and the need to define and understand the nature of evil grew, Beelzebub became a prominent figure in Christian demonology, often depicted as one of the chief lieutenants of Satan or even as an aspect of Satan himself. In medieval texts, such as the "Inferno" by Dante Alighieri and later in the writings of John Milton's "Paradise Lost," Beelzebub is portrayed as a fallen angel, second only to Satan in the hierarchy of hell. This depiction aligns with the Christian cosmology of a structured underworld, where demons serve as mirrors to the angels, each with defined roles and attributes.

During the witch hunts and the height of the demonological literature in Europe, Beelzebub was often invoked as a central figure in witches' sabbaths and demonic pacts. The "Malleus Maleficarum," a treatise on witchcraft from the late 15th century, describes Beelzebub as a mastermind of sorcery and maleficent acts, highlighting his role in medieval society as a symbol of ultimate evil, sedition against the divine order, and moral decay.

Modern interpretations of Beelzebub often reflect his origins as a lord of flies, associating him with decay, corruption, and disease. His role in contemporary religious and pop culture varies, from being a metaphor for the human propensity towards evil to a character in horror films and literature, representing the fascination and horror that the concept of ultimate evil inspires.

The Nephilim

The Nephilim, enigmatic figures of Judeo-Christian mythology, appear in several ancient texts, most notably the Hebrew Bible. Delving into the origins, descriptions, and the theological and cultural significance of the Nephilim provides insight into how ancient cultures viewed divine-human interactions and the moral complexities surrounding them.

The primary biblical reference to the Nephilim is found in Genesis 6:1-4, a passage that precedes the story of Noah's Ark. According to this account, the Nephilim were the offspring of the "sons of God" and the "daughters of men." The text describes them as "the heroes of old, men of renown." This ambiguous description has led to various interpretations: some view the "sons of God" as angels who descended to Earth, breaking divine laws by marrying human women and producing the Nephilim. Others interpret these "sons" as descendants of Seth, representing a lineage of pious men who mingled with the less virtuous descendants of Cain, leading to moral degradation represented by their offspring.

The term "Nephilim" is traditionally translated as "giants," derived from the Hebrew root "npl," meaning "to fall." This translation has fed into interpretations that suggest the Nephilim were not only physically gigantic but also "fallen" in a moral or spiritual sense. The presence of such beings is considered by some religious scholars as a catalyst for the Great Flood, their creation marking an irrevocable corruption of human flesh and spirit, necessitating divine intervention to reset the moral compass of humanity.

The Nephilim are also mentioned in the Book of Numbers when the Israelite spies report back to Moses about the land of Canaan: "We saw the Nephilim there (the descendants of Anak come from the Nephilim). We seemed like grasshoppers in our own eyes, and we looked the same to them." This reference connects the Nephilim with the Anakim, suggesting a lineage of formidable beings who instilled fear and perceived as insurmountable obstacles to the Israelites' conquest of Canaan.

Beyond the biblical texts, the Nephilim figure prominently in various apocryphal and pseudepigraphal works, most notably the Book of Enoch. This text expands significantly on the brief Genesis account, providing detailed narratives about the Watchers—angels who father the Nephilim. According to Enoch, the Watchers teach humanity various arts and technologies, such as weaponry and cosmetics, which some traditions interpret as forbidden knowledge that accelerates humanity's moral decay.

Theological interpretations of the Nephilim reflect broader questions about the nature of righteousness, the propagation of evil, and divine justice. In these interpretations, the Nephilim are often seen as an aberration, a violation of the intended order of creation that directly challenges the boundaries set by God for created beings. Their narrative is thus a prelude to themes of divine retribution and grace that are central to the Flood narrative.

Culturally, the Nephilim have permeated modern media and literature, appearing in books, movies, and video games, often depicted as formidable warriors or tragic figures caught between two worlds.

Exorcism and Demonic Possession

The concept of demonic possession—wherein a malevolent entity inhabits and takes control of a person—has been acknowledged in various forms throughout Christian history. Similarly, exorcism, the religious or spiritual practice of evicting demons from a person perceived to be possessed, is not only a ritualistic response but also a theological assertion of divine power over evil.

Historical Context

The belief in spirits, both benevolent and malevolent, was common in pre-Christian religions and integrated into Christian thought through the early Church Fathers. The New Testament contains several accounts of Jesus casting out demons as part of his ministry, providing a scriptural basis that has influenced Christian understanding of possession and exorcism. For instance, the Gospels of Matthew, Mark, and Luke describe multiple instances of Jesus confronting and expelling demons, often with a simple command or prayer. This authority over demons was also granted to his disciples as a sign of divine power and a testament to the truth of Jesus' mission.

Theological Underpinnings

In Christian theology, demonic possession is often seen as the result of spiritual warfare between the forces of good, led by God and his angels, and the forces of evil, led by Satan and his demons. This duality reflects the broader theological theme of cosmic battle between divine and satanic forces. Possession is considered one of the most explicit manifestations of this conflict, where human souls are the battleground.

Exorcism, therefore, is not merely a ritual but a declaration of faith and an enactment of divine authority. It is predicated on the belief that through prayer and specific ritual actions, exercised by an ordained minister or an individual granted special charisms, the Church can intervene on behalf of the possessed individual, compelling the demon to leave by the power of Christ.

Development of Exorcism Rites

The rites of exorcism have evolved significantly over centuries. The early Christian approach was relatively simple, often involving the laying on of hands, prayers, and the sign of the cross. As the medieval period progressed, exorcism became more formalized, particularly with the rise of monasticism and the increased focus on ritual purity.

By the time of the Renaissance, the Roman Ritual (Rituale Romanum) codified exorcism practices in 1614 under Pope Paul V. This codification included detailed instructions, prayers, and practices meant to ensure the efficacy and safety of the exorcism process. The Roman Ritual was the standard Catholic exorcism manual until it was revised after the Second Vatican Council, reflecting both a theological and a pastoral response to the understanding of possession and exorcism.

Exorcism in Practice

Exorcism practices vary widely across Christian denominations. The Catholic Church requires a thorough investigation before an exorcism is performed, often involving psychiatric evaluations to rule out mental illness, which the Church distinguishes from genuine demonic possession. Only priests with specific permission from a bishop can perform an exorcism, using the revised Rite of Exorcism that emphasizes the prayerful support of the Church and the power of Christ.

Protestant denominations generally approach exorcism with less formality. Some charismatic and evangelical groups embrace a more spontaneous form of exorcism, often conducted within community prayer services without the extensive ritual framework observed by the Catholic Church. These practices emphasize personal faith and the community's collective prayer as mechanisms for delivering the possessed.

Cultural Impact and Modern Perspectives

The portrayal of exorcism in popular media often sensationalizes the practice, focusing on dramatic, visual manifestations of possession and exorcism. Films like "The Exorcist" have significantly influenced public perceptions, sometimes blurring the theological and psychological nuances involved in real-life cases.

In modern times, the practice of exorcism faces both skepticism and scrutiny. While some view it as a necessary spiritual intervention, others criticize it as a misinterpretation of psychological disorders. The Church maintains that genuine cases of possession are rare and that the ritual of exorcism, when needed, is a solemn and serious affair.

Demons in Islamic Texts

The Islamic world hosts a rich tapestry of cultural interpretations concerning dark creatures, primarily revolving around jinn and other supernatural entities. These interpretations not only reflect religious beliefs but also integrate regional folklore and societal norms, illustrating how such figures can influence and be influenced by the cultural settings in which they are imagined. Beliefs in dark creatures also serve psychological and social functions. They provide explanations for inexplicable or misfortunate events and serve as a means of social control, encouraging adherence to cultural norms and religious practices under the guise of avoiding supernatural retribution.

Jinn

The concept of jinn, integral to Islamic theology and Arab folklore. Unlike angels and demons as understood in Christian tradition, jinn are unique in their moral ambiguity and their ability to choose between good and evil.

The term "jinn" is derived from the Arabic root 'j-n-n,' meaning 'to hide' or 'to adapt,' reflecting their invisible nature or ability to appear in various forms. The Quran, the holy book of Islam, provides the primary theological basis for beliefs about jinn. They are mentioned in several chapters, indicating that like humans, they are creatures of

God, created from smokeless fire, in contrast to humans, who are made from clay.

Jinn are endowed with free will, enabling them to make moral choices and to be held accountable in the afterlife, much like humans. This capability to choose their path aligns them closely with human beings, setting them apart from angels who are purely obedient beings without free will. The Quran explicitly states that jinn, like humans, are subject to God's judgment and can be followers of any faith, including Islam. Some jinn are good, practicing Muslims, while others may reject faith and act maliciously towards humans.

In Islamic theology, jinn are considered part of the unseen world (al-Ghaib). Their existence is a significant aspect of Islamic cosmology, bridging the material and spiritual worlds. The Prophet Muhammad is said to have been sent as a prophet to both humans and jinn, and there are numerous hadiths (sayings of the Prophet) that discuss encounters between jinn and humans, including stories where jinn converted to Islam after hearing the Quran.

The ability of jinn to interact with the physical world and their moral ambiguity are sources of various myths and stories in Islamic culture. They are often depicted as living parallel to humans, with their own societies, laws, and orders. Jinn can marry, have children, eat, drink, and die, but their lives are generally longer and their abilities far greater than those of humans. They can move quickly, change shape, and they have the power to become invisible.

Beyond religious texts, jinn frequently appear in Middle Eastern and South Asian folklore, where they are central characters in countless stories, including many in "One Thousand and One Nights" (commonly known as "Arabian Nights"). In these tales, jinn might be benevolent or malevolent, and they often wield magical powers that can alter the courses of human lives. Their portrayal ranges from frightening tricksters to powerful guardians, and they are often invoked in magical rites and amulets to harness their powers for protection or to cure illness.

The character of Iblis (Satan), who refused to bow to Adam and was subsequently cast out of heaven, is sometimes associated with the jinn, though interpretations vary. In some traditions, Iblis is considered a jinn, while in others, he is a unique creation.

In contemporary contexts, beliefs in jinn continue to influence cultural practices across Muslim-majority countries. Reports of jinn possession and their exorcism might parallel beliefs in demonic possession in other religions, reflecting a broader human concern with the influence of unseen forces.

The Ifrit - Flames of the Ancient World

Among the many supernatural beings that populate Islamic mythology, the Ifrit stands out as particularly formidable and awe-inspiring. These creatures are often depicted in Islamic lore as a class of infernal jinn, formed from the smokeless flames, and are known for their strength, cunning, and a propensity to rebel against the order of the cosmos. The Ifrit's role in Islamic narratives is not merely to serve as a foil to the human protagonists but to challenge them, test their wits, and ultimately act as a measure of their moral fiber and spiritual strength.

The Ifrit, as described in Islamic texts, including the Quran, belongs to the jinn, entities created by Allah from a smokeless and scorching fire. The Quran discusses their existence in several verses, notably emphasizing their creation and their invisibility to humans, underscoring their place in the cosmic hierarchy as beings free to make choices, much like humans, and thus capable of both righteousness and sin.

The origins of Ifrits are steeped in the pre-Islamic traditions of the Middle East. They are often thought to embody the spirits of the dead, particularly those who died in a state of sin or grievance. Over time, these entities have been integrated into Islamic eschatology as creatures possessing free will, thus capable of conversion to Islam or continuation in their rebellion against divine order.

In folklore, Ifrits are typically portrayed as malevolent, powerful, and often vengeful spirits. Their depiction in the "One Thousand and One Nights," a famous collection of Middle Eastern folk tales, highlights their supernatural strength and often malicious intent. They are depicted as formidable opponents who can shape-shift, become invisible, and exercise great magical powers. Yet, these stories also show Ifrits as bound by certain magical or divine laws, which can be exploited by clever and pious individuals to outwit or overpower them.

The stories often revolve around an Ifrit's interaction with a human, usually a tale of conflict, trickery, or moral testing. For instance, in "The Fisherman and the Jinni," an Ifrit who has been imprisoned in a bottle tricks a poor fisherman into releasing him, only to threaten the man's life. The narrative unfolds with the fisherman using his wits to reimpose control over the Ifrit, demonstrating human resilience and cleverness in the face of raw supernatural power.

Philosophically, the Ifrit represents the chaotic and uncontrollable elements of the world that challenge the moral and spiritual order. They are often used in Islamic teachings as examples of the jinn who chose the path of pride and rebellion rather than submission to Allah. This choice makes the Ifrits symbols of the struggle against the nafs (self or ego) and the temptations that can lead one away from the path of righteousness.

Ifrits have permeated various aspects of Middle Eastern and Islamic culture, appearing in literature, films, and other forms of popular media. They embody the perpetual human fascination with the supernatural, serving as characters that bring stories of conflict, danger, and the supernatural to life.

Iblis

Iblis, a central figure in Islamic theology, embodies the themes of pride, rebellion, and the eternal consequences of defiance against divine authority. His story offers profound insights into the nature of free will, obedience, and the moral tests that face spiritual beings and humans alike within Islamic thought. Iblis's narrative contrasts sharply with Christian and Jewish interpretations of Satan, providing a distinct perspective on evil and its origins in Abrahamic religions.

In Islamic tradition, Iblis is commonly associated with the jinn, beings created from smokeless fire, distinct from angels who are made of light. This origin is significant as it underscores the Islamic view that jinn, like humans, possess free will—a trait that angels do not share. Iblis's fall from grace is primarily attributed to his refusal to bow to Adam when God commanded all the angels to do so. Iblis, considering himself superior because he was created from fire as opposed to Adam's clay, saw this act as beneath him. His refusal was based on pride and prejudice, leading to his downfall.

The Quran details this incident in several verses, where Iblis argues with God and justifies his disobedience. Rather than an immediate punishment, Iblis is granted a reprieve until the Day of Judgment, during which he vows to lead humans astray as proof of their unworthiness. This aspect of Iblis's story highlights the Islamic concept of divine justice and mercy, even when dealing with those who disobey God's commands.

Iblis's role extends beyond mere narrative; he embodies the struggle between good and evil inherent in the world. His presence allows for the moral testing of humans, providing them the opportunity to choose righteousness over sin. This dynamic is critical in Islamic teachings about the purpose of life on earth: the world is a field of testing, and Iblis is a necessary part of that test. His ability to tempt and deceive is balanced by the clear guidance and mercy provided by God through revelations and the prophets.

The story of Iblis emphasizes the importance of obedience and humility in Islam. It serves as a warning against the dangers of pride and prejudice. Iblis's refusal to bow to Adam was not just a refusal to honor a human being but a challenge to divine wisdom which ordained that all creation should show humility regardless of origin.

Iblis's story is often compared to that of Satan in Christian and Jewish traditions, but there are key differences. In Christianity, Satan is often seen as a fallen angel, not a jinn, and his fall is due to a self-initiated rebellion against God rather than a direct command to bow to humans. Furthermore, Iblis's dialogue with God after his disobedience shows a complex relationship in Islamic texts. While he defies God, he also acknowledges God's sovereignty and accepts the consequences of his actions.

In modern Muslim societies, Iblis is still a significant figure in the collective imagination, often invoked to explain personal and societal moral failings. Discussions about Iblis can also be found in contemporary theological debates about predestination and free will, the nature of evil, and the human capacity for redemption. Moreover, the figure of Iblis has been explored in various cultural products, including literature and film, where he is portrayed from multiple perspectives.

The Qareen - Shadows of the Self

Qareen stands out as a profound and intriguing aspect. This entity is not just a mere footnote in Islamic eschatology but a mirror to the duality of human nature, a constant companion from cradle to grave. The Qareen is an unseen being, a spiritual double of every individual, believed to be a part of the unseen world, which in Islamic doctrine is as real as the world we inhabit.

The Qareen is mentioned in the Quran, which provides an authoritative basis for its existence in Islamic belief. Specifically, in Surah Qaf (Chapter 50, Verse 27), the Qareen is implicated in the context of the Day of Judgment. It appears as a figure that argues against the human to whom it was attached, revealing the misdeeds and perhaps arguing about the shared culpability in those actions. This moment underscores the Islamic teaching that everyone is responsible for their choices, with the Qareen acting as a sort of devil's advocate, literally embodying the temptations and lower impulses of the human soul.

Islamic scholars often describe the Qareen as a type of jinn or demon, created from smokeless fire, and assigned to every human being. This pairing occurs at birth, and the Qareen follows its human counterpart throughout their life, whispering to them, urging them towards impulsive acts or evil deeds. However, unlike the Christian concept of a demon, the Qareen's role is not merely to tempt but also to test the strength of a person's faith and character.

The interactions between a person and their Qareen influence daily decisions. The theology here is intricate, as it interplays with the concepts of predestination and free will, central themes in Islamic thought. The presence of the Qareen challenges the individual to engage in a constant struggle against their lower desires. The greater the individual's awareness and resistance to the Qareen's influence, the stronger their faith and moral fortitude are presumed to be.

The shadow self consists of the repressed, denied, or unknown aspects of the personality. In many ways, the Qareen embodies this shadow, always present, a bearer of uncomfortable truths about oneself, and a provocateur leading one to confront these hidden aspects.

The concept also opens a window into understanding how pre-modern societies grappled with questions of consciousness and morality. The Qareen represents a tangible acknowledgment of the internal conflicts that rage within each person, the ongoing battle between higher aspirations and base instincts. In Islamic teachings, the ultimate success in life and the hereafter is predicated on one's ability to navigate this battlefield, to subdue one's Qareen by aligning more closely with divine will and the teachings of the Prophet Muhammad.

Tales often depict scenarios where a Qareen might become visible to someone other than their counterpart, especially if magical or mystical practices are involved. These stories, while not strictly canonical, illustrate the depth of the cultural integration of the Qareen into the everyday life and worldview of various Islamic societies.

The existence of a Qareen does not absolve individuals from the consequences of their choices; rather, it highlights the intrinsic challenges embedded within the human experience. Every whisper of misguidance from the Qareen is matched by a call from the angel on the opposite shoulder, advising good deeds and righteousness, reflecting the dual influences that tug at every human heart. In essence, the Qareen teaches that the path to spiritual enlightenment and moral integrity is fraught with internal challenges and that victory over one's lower self is a testament to the strength and purity of one's faith.

The Evil Eye and Protective Verses in Islam

In Islamic spiritual beliefs, the concept of the Evil Eye—known as 'al-'ayn' in Arabic—holds a significant place, intertwining the daily lives and spiritual practices of millions. It is a belief that certain individuals possess the ability to cause harm, intentionally or unintentionally, by a mere envious or malevolent glance. This concept, while prevalent in various forms across different cultures, is deeply embedded in Islamic teachings, which also provide methods for protection against such malevolent forces.

The Evil Eye is considered a potent force in Islamic culture, and its effects are taken seriously among Muslim communities worldwide. The belief is that envy can be so powerful that it brings about actual harm to the object of such sentiments, be it a person, animal, or even an inanimate object. Symptoms of affliction by the Evil Eye include unexplained poor health, loss of appetite, excessive yawning, fatigue, and other maladies without apparent physical cause.

This concern with the Evil Eye is not purely cultural. It is supported and augmented by religious texts and practices. References to the Evil Eye in Islamic scripture can be primarily found in the Hadiths, the records of the sayings and actions of the Prophet Muhammad. For instance, Sahih Muslim, one of the principal Hadith collections, includes references where the Prophet acknowledges the reality of the Evil Eye and advises his followers to recite certain verses from the Quran to seek protection.

The Quran itself, while not explicitly mentioning the Evil Eye, contains verses that are widely used to seek protection against harm. Among these, Surah Al-Falaq (Chapter 113) and Surah An-Nas (Chapter 114) are particularly significant. These chapters are collectively known as the Mu'awwidhat or "Verses of Refuge" and are recited for protection against various types of evils, including the malicious intent manifested through the Evil Eye.

Surah Al-Falaq begins with an invocation to the Lord of the dawn, seeking refuge from the evil of created things, the darkness when it spreads, and from the evil of the envier when he envies. This particular verse encapsulates the Islamic remedy to the dangers posed by envy and malice. Surah An-Nas, on the other hand, seeks protection from the whisperings of the sneaking whisperer, who whispers into the hearts of mankind. Together, these Surahs encompass protection against external physical and psychological threats.

In addition to the recitation of these Surahs, various Hadiths prescribe practical measures against the Evil Eye, such as the use of the phrase "Masha'Allah" (What God has willed) to acknowledge that all virtues and possessions come from God and are under His will. This expression is believed to help in preventing the arousal of envy.

While Muslims believe in the ultimate power and control of Allah over all things, there is also a recognition of the existence of evil forces which can influence human affairs. Prophet Muhammad recommended the use of protective amulets that adhere to Islamic teachings, such as writings of the Quranic verses. He particularly endorsed the practice of bathing as a remedy for those afflicted by the Evil Eye. The method involves using the water from the one who is believed to have caused the Evil Eye, believing that it can reverse the harmful effects.

Evil Eye influences social behaviors, guiding how people display their blessings and achievements, often with caution and modesty to avoid invoking the envy of others. It is common in Muslim societies to downplay one's success or to frequently credit Allah for personal achievements as a way to ward off potential envy.

Dark Creatures of Japanese Folklore

In the shadowy corners of Japanese folklore, myriad creatures lurk, embodying the fears and superstitions of a culture steeped in mystery and ritual. These beings, often malevolent and always enigmatic, are not just figments of imagination but are integral to the understanding of the darker aspects of the human psyche as perceived by traditional Japanese beliefs.

Yokai

The term 'Yokai' is often translated as "ghost" or "monster" but these words only scratch the surface of the complexities and nuances associated with these beings. Yokai can take on countless forms, from animals and humanoids to inanimate objects that have come to life after achieving great age and gaining magical powers, a concept known as 'tsukumogami'. The diversity in their appearances and behaviors reflects the rich tapestry of local beliefs and the human tendency to personify natural events and societal fears.

Historically, Yokai were thought to be responsible for various misfortunes — diseases, natural disasters, and other inexplicable phenomena. In ancient Japan, explaining away sudden illness or misfortune as the work of Yokai was a way to make sense of the world's randomness and cruelty. Over time, these beliefs were compiled in encyclopedias of the supernatural, such as the famous "Gazu Hyakki Yagyō" (The Illustrated Night Parade of a Hundred Demons) by Toriyama Sekien in the 18th century. These works, while serving to catalog the myriad forms of Yokai, also reflect the period's fascination with the supernatural, blending folk beliefs with emerging urban culture.

One of the most iconic Yokai is the 'Kappa', a water creature known for challenging humans to sumo wrestling and for its mischievous behavior, including pulling unsuspecting people into rivers. Another popular Yokai is the 'Tengu', the mountain and forest dwelling creatures known for their interaction with the warriors and monks, as previously discussed. Then there are the 'Oni', typically portrayed as large and menacing with horns and ogre-like features, often associated with the punishment of the wicked in Hell.

Yokai not only serve to explain the natural world but also to enforce moral standards and social norms. Many stories depict them punishing those who break societal rules, highlighting themes of justice and retribution. For example, the 'Rokurokubi', women whose necks stretch at night, often prey on those who wander alone at night, embodying the consequences of straying from the path both literally and metaphorically.

In addition to their roles in folklore, Yokai have been subjects of various forms of art and literature throughout Japanese history. During the Edo period, the portrayal of Yokai shifted from fear-inducing tales to more humorous and whimsical narratives, reflecting changes in societal attitudes towards these creatures. This transformation can be seen in the works of artists like Utagawa Kuniyoshi, who depicted Yokai with a playful, often satirical tone, engaging audiences with both visual and narrative creativity.

The influence of Yokai extends into contemporary Japanese culture, where they appear in manga, anime, and films, often as key characters. These modern portrayals sometimes maintain the traditional attributes of the Yokai while also adapting them to fit contemporary themes and narratives.

Yokai festivals and events also play a significant role in keeping the traditions alive, particularly in regions known for their historical connections to these stories. These events often feature parades, Yokai-themed art exhibitions, and performances, fostering a sense of community and cultural continuity.

Oni – Demons of Japanese Folklore

The Oni, a significant and fearsome figure in Japanese folklore, manifests across various forms of literature, art, and cultural traditions, symbolizing the darker aspects of existence and human nature. These supernatural beings, often depicted as demons or ogres, have captivated the imagination of people throughout Japanese history, embodying the consequences of vice and the presence of malevolence in the world.

Traditionally, Oni are portrayed as hideous, towering creatures with wild hair, horns, and fanged teeth, their bodies covered in scales or coarse fur. Their appearance, marked by vivid colors, typically red or blue skin, and carrying iron clubs or kanabō, strikes fear and warns of the brute strength and malevolent intent they possess. This fearsome depiction serves as a visual caution against evil and is a stark representation of the punishment that awaits those who succumb to wickedness.

The etymology of the word 'Oni' is often associated with the kanji for "to hide or conceal," suggesting that Oni could represent the hidden or chaotic passions within humans. In Japanese folklore, Oni frequently start as human beings who transform into these monstrous beings as a result of extreme evil or wicked emotions, such as jealousy or anger. This transformation illustrates a central theme in Japanese mythology: the consequences of letting base emotions control one's actions.

Oni appear predominantly in Japanese folklore and myth as antagonists involved in stories where they terrorize villages, kidnap maidens, challenge heroes, and guard Hell's gates. One of the most famous tales involving an Oni is the story of Momotaro, the Peach Boy, who confronts and defeats a band of Oni on a distant island, liberating their captives and returning with their treasure. This narrative not only entertains but also serves to instruct in virtue and courage, emphasizing the societal values of bravery and righteousness.

In the Buddhist context, Oni are often seen as punishers of the damned in Hell, a role that aligns them with the idea of justice and retribution. They are the executors of divine punishment, a concept that underscores the moral of actions having consequences.

The duality of Oni is further explored in rituals and festivals, most notably during Setsubun, the day before the beginning of spring according to the Japanese lunar calendar. During Setsubun, it is customary to throw roasted soybeans either out the door or at a member of the family wearing an Oni mask, while shouting "Oni wa soto! Fuku wa uchi!" ("Demons out! Luck in!"). This ritual, known as mamemaki, symbolizes the expulsion of evil and misfortune and the welcoming of happiness and prosperity. It reflects the belief that human actions can influence spiritual realities, encouraging cleanliness, and morality to ensure the favor of the gods.

Oni are not universally evil. In some tales, they can be benevolent or protective if respected or appeased. For example, the Oni of Rashomon Gate, who was famously defeated by the heroic Minamoto no Yorimitsu, later became his protector. Such stories suggest that Oni, much like humans, are capable of change and redemption, adding a layer of complexity to their character within Japanese mythology. Their dramatic portrayal in these traditional performances reinforces their role in popular culture as symbols of that which must be overcome—be it internal conflict or external adversity.

Tengu - The Mystical Protectors of the Mountains

In the pantheon of Japanese mythology, Tengu stand out as among the most enigmatic and multifaceted creatures. These legendary beings have transitioned through centuries from harbingers of war to protectors of the Dharma (Buddhist teachings), reflecting significant shifts in their cultural and religious significance. Originating in Japanese folklore, Tengu are often depicted with human and avian characteristics, symbolizing their connection to both the earthly realm and spiritual domains.

Historically, Tengu were thought to be disruptive demons and harbingers of war. Early depictions show them as bird-like creatures, which over time evolved into more human forms with long noses or beaks and red faces, embodying their supernatural essence and fearsome nature. This transformation in their physical depiction parallels their changing role in Japanese folklore and religion.

Tengu are primarily associated with the Shugendō tradition, a syncretic form of Buddhist and Shinto mountain asceticism that emphasizes the importance of physical endurance as a path to spiritual power. Practitioners, known as Yamabushi, often considered Tengu both as protectors and as tests of their faith and resolve. According to legends, Tengu possess deep knowledge of the martial arts, which they could impart to worthy warriors or monks, making them respected figures among samurai and martial artists.

One of the most famous legends involving Tengu is the tale of the warrior monk Saitō Musashibō Benkei. It is said that as a young man, Benkei was taught by the Tengu of Kurama Mountain, from whom he learned the art of swordsmanship and tactics that later defined his legendary military prowess. This story highlights the Tengu's role not only as martial experts but also as teachers of lost or secret knowledge, bridging the human world and the spiritual.

In addition to their martial prowess, Tengu are considered custodians of the forest and mountains. They are believed to have the ability to move through the woods without a trace and to speak the language of the forest, communicating with trees and animals. Their deep connection with nature underscores their role as protectors of the environment, serving as a reminder of the consequences of disrespecting natural spaces.

The dual nature of Tengu—sometimes benevolent, sometimes malevolent—is reflective of their origin story in Buddhist mythology, which suggests they were once proud, vain priests who, because of their arrogance, were reborn as Tengu. This origin reflects the Buddhist theme of karma and transformation, with Tengu serving as a cautionary tale against the dangers of spiritual pride and the potential for redemption.

Tengu are often depicted in iconography carrying the Shakujo (a ringed staff used by Buddhist monks) and the Ha-uchiwa (feather fan). These items symbolize their authority and mystical powers, such as the ability to stir great winds or to create illusions. In contemporary adaptations, Tengu are often portrayed as complex figures, sometimes as noble guardians, other times as mischievous tricksters, always maintaining their intrinsic connection to the spiritual and natural world.

Kitsune - The Divine and the Cunning

Kitsune, the Japanese word for fox, is not just an animal in Japanese folklore but a multifaceted symbol of cunning, complexity, and supernatural attributes. Kitsune are venerated as intelligent beings possessing magical abilities, most notably the power to transform into human form. These creatures inhabit a significant place in Shinto religion as messengers and servants of the deities, yet they also appear in countless folktales as tricksters, bridging the sacred with the profane, the divine with the earthly.

The reverence of Kitsune is closely associated with Inari, the Shinto deity of rice, fertility, and prosperity. Kitsune are considered Inari's messengers and are believed to have the ability to ward off evil spirits. Statues of Kitsune, often depicted holding a key or a jewel in their mouths, are a common sight at Inari shrines, symbolizing their role as protectors and benefactors. This divine aspect highlights their benevolent nature and their integral role in Shinto practices, where they are seen as bringers of good fortune and success.

Conversely, Kitsune also feature prominently in Japanese folklore as cunning beings with a penchant for causing chaos and trickery. These stories often depict them using their transformative abilities to deceive humans, sometimes out of malice but often as a test of character or as a form of playful mischief. For example, a common tale recounts a Kitsune transforming into a beautiful woman who tricks a proud samurai, teaching him a lesson in humility and respect.

Kitsune are believed to grow in power as they age and increase in wisdom. A young Kitsune may have only one tail, but as they grow older, they can develop up to nine tails. A nine-tailed Kitsune, or Kyubi no Kitsune, is considered especially powerful and wise, having lived for thousands of years. This idea of multiple tails signifying age and wisdom is unique to Kitsune and underscores their mystical and elusive nature.

The ability of Kitsune to shift between forms has deep symbolic meanings. This transformation is not just physical but represents the fluidity and ambiguity of reality and perception. Kitsune challenge the boundaries between human and animal, spirit and physical form, illustrating the complex interplay between nature and the supernatural. In this capacity, they serve as a metaphor for change and the unexpected, embodying the idea that things are not always as they seem.

Kitsune are also associated with the concept of Kitsunetsuki, the state of being possessed by a fox. Traditionally, this was believed to cause bizarre behavior and was often used to explain various illnesses or mental disturbances.

In addition to their spiritual and mythical roles, Kitsune have a significant presence in contemporary Japanese culture. They appear in modern literature, anime, and films, often embodying characteristics from traditional folklore while adapting to contemporary narratives. In these settings, Kitsune often explore themes of identity, transformation, and the supernatural, bridging historical beliefs with modern existential questions. The duality of Kitsune is celebrated in annual festivals across Japan, where participants wear fox masks and partake in rituals that honor both their divine and trickster aspects.

Yuki-onna - The Spirit of Winter

Yuki-onna, the "Snow Woman," is a captivating figure in Japanese mythology, representing the perilous beauty of winter. As one of the most renowned and enigmatic Yokai, or supernatural entities in Japanese folklore, Yuki-onna embodies the dual nature of winter: its serene beauty and its deadly hazards. Her legends vary widely across Japan, reflecting the diverse cultural perceptions of snow and winter that differ by region.

Yuki-onna often appears in stories as a tall, beautiful woman with long black hair and blue lips, her skin inhumanly pale or even transparent, blending seamlessly with the snowy landscape. She is sometimes seen wearing a white kimono, but other legends describe her as nude, veiled only by the falling snow. This visual portrayal emphasizes her connection to winter and her role as both a serene and treacherous presence.

The origins of Yuki-onna are not well-documented, which adds to her mystique. She is thought to embody the spirit of snow and is often associated with snowy, mountainous regions of Japan where she appears to travelers caught in blizzards. Her interactions with humans are marked by both malevolence and mercy, which underscores the unpredictable nature of winter and the spirits that inhabit it.

In many tales, Yuki-onna has the power to freeze people to death, and she uses this ability without pity or remorse. One popular story describes her sparing a young man with the condition that he never speaks of their encounter; years later, he breaks his vow and she returns not to kill him, but to take away his beloved children, reflecting the theme of broken promises and the harsh reprisals of nature.

However, Yuki-onna is not always portrayed as purely malevolent. In some stories, she shows a capacity for love and other human emotions. A well-known variant depicts her marrying a mortal man and bearing his children, only to disappear after her husband discovers her true nature. This version of the story highlights her connection to human society and her struggle between her nature as a spirit and her fleeting desire for human warmth and companionship.

The ambivalent nature of Yuki-onna in folklore reflects broader themes in human interaction with the natural world, particularly the awe and fear that severe weather can inspire. Snow, in these stories, is both a source of beauty and a potential deadly trap, and Yuki-onna personifies this duality. She is the winter that can enchant the eyes even as it numbs the flesh.

Yuki-onna also plays a significant role in Japanese arts and literature, inspiring numerous adaptations and interpretations in film, literature, and animations. These portrayals often explore the themes of isolation, loneliness, and the stark beauty of winter, all attributes embodied by Yuki-onna. Her story is a poignant reminder of the power of nature and the spiritual qualities that people have historically attributed to natural phenomena.

Yuki-onna's tales are often used as cautionary tales that warn against venturing into danger and the importance of respecting the forces of nature, which can be as ruthless as they are beautiful. This respect for nature is a key element of Shinto, Japan's indigenous spirituality, which often emphasizes harmony with the natural world. Cultural activities and festivals in regions known for heavy snowfalls sometimes include references to Yuki-onna, serving as a cultural expression of the communities' relationship with winter and its impact on their lives.

Norse Mythology's Dark Beings

Norse mythology, with its gods, heroes, and monsters, presents a vivid panorama of the ancient Norse worldview, filled with stark dualities and profound depth. Within this mythological corpus, there are beings who embody the darker, more malevolent forces of the universe. These entities are not merely evil; they are complex figures that represent chaos, destruction, and the necessary counterpoints to the order and prosperity brought by the gods.

Hel - The Goddess of the Underworld

In Norse mythology, Hel is a central figure in the pantheon of gods and creatures, ruling over the eponymous realm of the dead, Helheim. Unlike many mythological traditions where the underworld is a place of torment and punishment, Helheim is depicted more neutrally, as a final resting place for those who did not die in battle but from illness or old age. Hel, as the goddess of this realm, is often portrayed as a being with a dual nature, reflecting the dualities of life and death, and decay and regeneration.

Hel is described in the medieval texts, particularly the Prose Edda and the Poetic Edda, which are the primary sources for what we know about Norse mythology. According to these texts, Hel is the daughter of the trickster god Loki and the giantess Angrboda, making her part of a family of powerful and often troubling figures. Her siblings include Fenrir, the great wolf, and Jörmungandr, the world serpent, each of whom plays a significant role in Norse cosmology. Her lineage alone sets her apart as a formidable entity in the mythological hierarchy.

The physical description of Hel is notably striking and emblematic of her role as the overseer of the realm of the dead. She is often depicted as half alive and half dead, with one side of her body resembling a living woman, while the other side appears decayed and ghastly. This duality symbolizes her dominion over the threshold between life and death, making her a complex figure who embodies the inescapable nature of mortality.

Hel's realm, Helheim, is located in the far north, a cold and dreary place, yet it is not a realm of punishment but rather one of continuation after life. The souls who reside there do not suffer torment; instead, they exist in a shadowy version of their earthly life. This nuanced view of the afterlife reflects the Norse cultural perception of death as a natural and inevitable phase of existence rather than a consequence of moral failings.

In mythology, Hel's character is pivotal in several key stories, including the events leading to Ragnarok, the end of the world in Norse mythology. One of the most significant narratives involving Hel is the death of the god Baldr. After Baldr is killed due to Loki's machinations, Hel receives his soul in her realm. The gods, wishing to revive Baldr, send an emissary to negotiate his release. Hel agrees to free Baldr on the condition that all things, living and dead, weep for him. This condition is nearly met, save for one giantess, often thought to be Loki in disguise, who refuses to cry, thereby sealing Baldr's fate.

The figure of Hel in Norse mythology is not merely a goddess of death but also a symbol of the inevitability and impartiality of death. Her dominion over Helheim is critical for maintaining the balance between the worlds of the living and the dead. This role can be seen as reflecting the Norse understanding of the cosmos as governed by laws and balances, with Hel as a custodian of these cosmic scales.

Furthermore, Hel's imagery and symbolism have permeated various aspects of modern culture, influencing literature, art, and media. Her depiction as a goddess who is both part of the realm of the gods and a ruler of the underworld has made her a figure of fascination and contemplation, often representing themes of transition, boundaries, and the interplay between life and death.

Hel challenges the often binary perception of death found in many other religious or mythological systems. In Norse culture, death is a more complex and layered experience, not confined to ideas of heaven and hell but rather seen as a continuation of existence in a different form. Hel, as both a guardian and a ruler of this profound aspect of human existence, invites a deeper reflection on the nature of life and death and the values that define them.

Loki - The Enigmatic Trickster

Loki, a pivotal figure in Norse mythology, embodies the complexities of deceit, transformation, and chaos. His role is not confined to that of a mere trickster; he is also a shape-shifter, a problem solver, and at times, a bringer of necessary, though harsh, truths. This complexity makes Loki one of the most intriguing and multifaceted figures in Norse lore.

Loki is often described as the son of the giant Farbauti and the giantess Laufey, and he is frequently referred to as the "blood-brother" of Odin, the chief of the Norse gods. This kinship with Odin integrates Loki into the Aesir, the principal tribe of Norse gods, granting him a unique position among both gods and giants. His dual lineage allows him to navigate both worlds, often acting as a go-between, which is crucial in many mythological narratives.

The myths describe Loki as a master of guile and deception, possessing the ability to change his shape and even his gender. His transformations are numerous; he has turned into a salmon, a mare, a fly, and even a woman—the mother of Odin's eight-legged horse Sleipnir, underscoring his role as a boundary-crosser and norm challenger. Each transformation has significant outcomes, affecting gods and mortals alike, and often leading to profound changes in the cosmic order.

Loki's actions are not always malevolent; in many tales, he is depicted as helping the gods with clever solutions to seemingly insurmountable problems. However, his assistance often comes at a price, and his motives are rarely straightforward. This ambiguity is a hallmark of his character, reflecting the Norse appreciation for cunning and intellect even when they lead to disorder.

One of the most famous myths involving Loki is the story of the death of Baldr, the beloved son of Odin and Frigg. Baldr's death, orchestrated by Loki, sets off a chain of events leading to Ragnarok, the end of the world as prophesied in Norse mythology. Loki tricks another god into killing Baldr with mistletoe, the only material that can harm him. This act of betrayal reveals Loki's capacity for spite and destruction, significantly altering the dynamics among the Aesir and setting the stage for the final cataclysmic battle.

Despite his pivotal role in causing Baldr's death, Loki's actions are not solely destructive. In some stories, he is portrayed as exposing the gods' arrogance and hypocrisy, challenging the status quo and forcing the gods to confront their shortcomings. This aspect of Loki as a catalyst for change, though often painful and chaotic, is essential for transformation and renewal within the mythological framework.

Loki's eventual punishment by the gods—being bound beneath the earth with a serpent's venom dripping onto him until Ragnarok—is a testament to the gods' ambivalence towards him. His punishment is as extreme as his actions, reflecting the deep contradictions and tensions he embodies.

Loki's character has been the subject of various interpretations in modern media and literature, highlighting his enduring appeal. He is often seen as a symbol of the rebel, challenging authority and conventional morality, which resonates in contemporary narratives that value individuality and questioning of traditional norms.

In Norse culture, where survival was paramount, and moral absolutes were less emphasized, Loki's traits of cunning and survival instinct were sometimes as valuable as the more straightforward heroism of other gods like Thor. His stories convey complex ethical lessons, where the outcomes of his schemes force a reflection on the consequences of actions, the nature of loyalty, and the inevitability of change.

Fenrir - The Bound Beast

Few figures are as tragic and formidable as Fenrir, the great wolf. A central figure in the lore that encapsulates themes of prophecy, fate, and the inescapable nature of destiny, Fenrir's story is interwoven with the very fabric of the Norse cosmological end known as Ragnarok.

Fenrir is one of the three children of the god Loki and the giantess Angrboda, making him a part of a progeny that includes Hel, the overseer of the underworld, and Jormungandr, the world-encircling sea serpent. From his birth, Fenrir was marked by prophecies that foretold his growth into a beast of unstoppable strength and ferocity. The gods, aware of these prophecies, faced a paradox. Fenrir's existence was woven into the fate of the world, yet his destined role was to bring about destruction, including the deaths of the gods themselves.

The narrative of Fenrir is deeply entwined with themes of trust and betrayal. As a pup, he was raised among the gods themselves, growing larger and stronger with each passing day. The gods, growing fearful yet wishing to avoid the direct killing of one of their kin, decided to bind Fenrir.

However, aware of his growing strength and the prophecies surrounding him, Fenrir became wary of their intentions. In an act that combines elements of cunning and desperation, the gods proposed a game to Fenrir to test the strength of various bindings, under the guise of a test of his strength.

When the gods presented Fenrir with the magical ribbon Gleipnir, claiming it was a test of his might, Fenrir was suspicious. He agreed to let them bind him only if one of the gods placed their hand in his mouth as a pledge of good faith. Tyr, the god of war and justice, agreed to this condition, showing a complex mixture of bravery and resignation to fate. When Fenrir found himself unable to break free from Gleipnir, he bit off Tyr's hand, fulfilling one part of his grim destiny and setting the stage for future betrayals and battles.

This moment of binding Fenrir not only reflects the Norse belief in the inescapability of fate but also explores the ethical dimensions of the gods' actions. Their decision to deceive and bind Fenrir, despite his having done no wrong, invites contemplation on themes of power, responsibility, and the ethical dilemmas.

Fenrir's binding can be seen as a metaphor for the suppression of chaotic and destructive forces, and his eventual breaking free during Ragnarok symbolizes the failure of such suppressive measures. At Ragnarok, Fenrir kills Odin, the chief of the gods, fulfilling the prophecy that the gods had long feared. This act of destruction, however, is not just an end but a part of the cycle of destruction and renewal that is central to Norse cosmology.

Fenrir's final battle with Odin's son, Vidar, who avenges his father by killing Fenrir, adds another layer to his mythological significance. This confrontation represents the themes of vengeance and the continuation of legacies within the divine families, highlighting the ongoing struggle between the forces of order and chaos.

Jörmungandr - The Midgard Serpent

In Norse mythology, Jörmungandr, also known as the Midgard Serpent, is a colossal sea serpent whose presence encapsulates the cyclical nature of creation and destruction, a recurring theme in the mythological narratives of the Norse people. As one of the three children of Loki and the giantess Angrboda, Jörmungandr stands alongside his siblings, Fenrir and Hel, as a central figure in the prophecies concerning Ragnarok, the end of the world.

From his birth, Jörmungandr was recognized by the gods as a threat due to the prophecies that foretold the havoc he would wreak upon the world. In an attempt to prevent these prophecies from coming to fruition, Odin, the chief of the Norse gods, threw Jörmungandr into the great ocean that encircles Midgard, the world of humans. The serpent grew so large that he was able to surround the earth and grasp his own tail, an act that symbolized the containment of chaos within the cosmic order. This image of Jörmungandr biting his own tail is rich with symbolic meaning, representing the concept of Ouroboros, an ancient symbol of eternal cyclic renewal or a cycle of life, death, and rebirth.

The existence of Jörmungandr serves as a constant reminder to the gods and to humanity of the fragile balance that holds the universe together. His presence in the seas also causes massive turbulence, influencing the other realms through storms and tidal waves, symbolizing his deep connection to the primal forces of nature and his role as an agent of change and destruction.

Jörmungandr's most notable mythological role occurs during Ragnarok, where he is destined to face Thor, the god of thunder. This epic confrontation was prophesied from the earliest times and is a pivotal event in the Norse eschatological framework. Throughout the mythology, Thor and Jörmungandr are archenemies, with several stories recounting their encounters. One of the most famous tales is their fishing expedition, where Thor, disguised as a young boy, accompanies the giant Hymir on a fishing trip. Thor attempts to pull Jörmungandr up from the ocean using an ox head as bait, but he is unable to complete the task when Hymir cuts the fishing line, fearing the destruction that might follow.

The ultimate battle between Thor and Jörmungandr at Ragnarok marks the climax of their enmity. In this cataclysmic event, Jörmungandr emerges from the sea, poisoning the sky and the waters with his venom. Thor succeeds in killing the great serpent but walks only nine steps before falling dead himself, poisoned by the serpent's venom. This mutual destruction is emblematic of the intertwined fate of all beings in Norse mythology — that all things must come to an end, only to be reborn in a new form.

In a broader cultural context, Jörmungandr symbolizes the boundless and often uncontrollable forces of nature that can both sustain and destroy life. His cyclic struggle with Thor reflects the perpetual conflict between order and chaos, a fundamental aspect of the Norse understanding of the universe. This battle also highlights the theme of heroism in Norse culture, where even the gods are not immune to death and must face their destiny with courage.

Draugar - The Undead of Norse Lore

In the shadowy corners of Norse mythology, few creatures are as chilling and complex as the Draugar, the undead beings that rise from their graves to protect their treasures or haunt the living. Unlike the benign spirits of some other cultural traditions, Draugar embody the darker aspects of the Norse afterlife, serving as a grim reminder of the fate that awaits those who are consumed by greed or unable to find rest due to unresolved issues in life.

The concept of the Draugr (singular of Draugar) originates in Old Norse literature, where these beings are described as reanimated corpses that possess supernatural strength, the ability to increase their size at will, and other ominous powers. Tales of the Draugar are found in the Icelandic sagas, particularly in those narratives that focus on the themes of vengeance, inheritance disputes, and the protection of burial sites. The Draugar's existence highlights the Norse belief in an active afterlife, where the dead can still influence the world of the living.

Draugar are typically portrayed as retaining some semblance of intelligence and possessing a physical form, often bloated and blackened, indicating their decayed state. They are capable of leaving their graves at night to visit the living, often spreading disease and death. The motivation for a Draugr's rise from the dead varies but often centers around protecting their grave sites from robbers or expressing unresolved envy and spite toward the living.

The burial practices of the Norse people reflect an acute awareness of the potential for the dead to return as Draugar. Graves were often constructed with elaborate measures, such as placing stones in the shape of a ship or using iron scissors to prevent the dead from rising. Additionally, corpses might be bound or even beheaded to further ensure they could not haunt the living.

One of the most famous stories involving a Draugr is that of Grettir the Strong from the Icelandic sagas. Grettir, known for his strength and bravery, encounters various Draugar throughout his adventures. In one notable episode, he confronts the Draugr known as Glámr, who had been terrorizing the local populace. The saga describes their fierce battle, which highlights Grettir's heroism and the formidable strength of the Draugr. Grettir ultimately overcomes Glámr, but not without receiving a curse from the dying Draugr that dooms Grettir's remaining days. This story not only emphasizes the physical danger posed by Draugar but also their ability to inflict psychological and spiritual suffering.

The Draugar's ability to curse the living is another aspect of their feared presence. These curses could manifest as bad luck, sickness, or even death, extending the Draugar's influence beyond their physical actions. This capability adds a layer of existential dread to the Draugr mythos, as it suggests that the dead can reach out with their bitterness or malevolence to alter the fates of the living.

In Norse culture, the stories of Draugar served multiple purposes. They were cautionary tales against the perils of greed and avarice, as the Draugar often guarded treasures buried with them in their mounds. They also provided moral lessons on the importance of resolving one's affairs before death and highlighted the belief that death was not an end but a continuation of existence in another form, subject to the deeds and misdeeds of one's earthly life.

Dark Creatures in Slavic Mythology

Slavic mythology, with its roots deeply embedded in the ancient forests and rugged landscapes of Eastern Europe, is replete with beings that embody the darker aspects of nature and human existence. These creatures, often stemming from the same archetypal origins as those in Western European folklore, bring their unique flavors to the myths and legends of the Slavic peoples.

Chernobog

In the pantheon of Slavic mythology, few figures are as mysterious and compelling as Chernobog, the god of darkness, misfortune, and woe. His name, derived from the Old East Slavic words cherno meaning "black" and bog meaning "god," directly translates to "Black God." Chernobog represents the darker aspects of the cosmos, serving as a stark counterpart to the brighter, more benevolent deities in Slavic religious belief.

Historical references to Chernobog are scant, but he is most notably mentioned in the Chronica Slavorum, a 12th century chronicle written by the German priest Helmold. In this text, Chernobog is described as a malevolent deity worshipped by the West Slavs, particularly during the times of the year associated with harvest's end and the onset of winter. This seasonal association aligns Chernobog with the death of nature and the hardships of winter, further solidifying his role as a deity of darkness and misfortune.

The characterization of Chernobog in Slavic mythology is primarily influenced by the dualistic belief system that pervades much of the region's folklore. In this system, cosmic balance is maintained through the opposition of good and evil forces. Chernobog's counterpart is often identified as Belobog, the "White God," a deity associated with light, goodness, and prosperity. This dichotomy between Chernobog and Belobog mirrors the natural cycles of day and night, summer and winter, growth and decay, reflecting the Slavic understanding of the world as a perpetual battleground of contrary forces.

Chernobog often conceived as a deity who oversees the domain of the dead, akin to Hades in Greek mythology. In this capacity, Chernobog is not only associated with the literal darkness of winter but also with the metaphysical darkness of death and the afterlife. This connection makes him an important figure in the eschatological and ritual aspects of Slavic religious practice, where appeasement of the darker forces represented a way to ensure harmony and balance within the community.

Despite his ominous nature, Chernobog's worship was not solely focused on fear or supplication. Instead, it involved a recognition of the necessity of dark and destructive forces in the world. Just as winter must come for spring to follow, Chernobog's influence was seen as a natural and essential aspect of the life cycle. Rituals and offerings to Chernobog, particularly during the winter solstice, can be seen as acknowledgments of his power and a means to placate him, ensuring that the period of darkness would eventually give way to light.

The image of Chernobog has also permeated Eastern European arts and literature, where he frequently appears as a symbol of ultimate evil or as a personification of the hardships faced by the people. His portrayal in these contexts often reflects historical and cultural anxieties, as well as a deep-seated recognition of the inevitability of suffering and misfortune in human life.

Chernobog helps articulate a fundamental truth about the human experience: that suffering and misfortune are integral to existence. His worship and the myths surrounding him serve as a means for people to confront and contextualize the inevitable challenges they face.

Koschei the Deathless

Koschei the Deathless is a prominent figure in Slavic folklore, embodying themes of immortality, the pursuit of power, and the moral consequences of evading death. Known also as Koschei the Immortal, his tales are steeped in the rich tradition of Eastern European mythology, serving as cautionary stories that explore the limits of human desire and the natural order of life and death.

Koschei's character is often portrayed as a menacing antagonist who kidnaps the hero's wife or beloved, sparking a series of quests and battles. Despite his fearsome reputation and seemingly invincible nature, his name, "Koschei," is derived from the Russian word kost, meaning "bone," suggesting a skeletal, death-like appearance that belies his inability to die. This paradoxical nature highlights the dual themes of decay and endurance that run through stories of Koschei.

The myth of Koschei the Deathless revolves around his secret to immortality. According to legend, Koschei's soul (or death) is hidden separate from his body inside a needle, which is in an egg, which is in a duck, which is in a hare, which is then locked in an iron chest. This chest is buried under a green oak tree on an island that is notoriously hard to find. This elaborate concealment of his life force serves as a metaphor for the lengths to which some will go to avoid death, and the complexity and fragility of such an endeavor.

Koschei's immortality, therefore, is his greatest strength, but also his ultimate weakness. The elaborate protection of his soul creates a vulnerability, which becomes a focal point in tales where the hero must find and destroy the needle to defeat him. This quest often requires cunning, bravery, and purity of heart, reflecting the virtues valued in Slavic cultures.

The tales of Koschei are not just stories of adventure and magic; they also carry deeper philosophical and moral questions about the nature of life and death. Koschei's choice to remove his death from his body can be seen as an unnatural act that goes against the ordained processes of the natural world, highlighting the dangers of tampering with life's cycle. Such themes resonate with universal concerns about mortality and the ethical implications of seeking to overcome it.

Koschei's interactions with other characters in these stories often reflect on themes of love, betrayal, and redemption. His frequent role as a kidnapper of heroes' wives or daughters may symbolize a corrupt desire to possess life or beauty, further emphasizing his detachment from the natural laws of existence. His defeat, usually at the hands of a young hero, symbolizes not only the triumph of good over evil but also the restoration of natural order and the reaffirmation of life cycles that include death.

Baba Yaga: The Witch

As a witch who dwells deep within the forest, Baba Yaga embodies the dual nature of the crone archetype: she is both a fearsome antagonist and a wise woman who provides guidance and magical assistance to those who prove themselves worthy.

The figure of Baba Yaga is most famously depicted living in a hut that stands on chicken legs, capable of rotating to face any direction. This hut, often described as surrounded by a fence made of human bones, signifies her connection to the supernatural and the otherworldly. The entrance to her dwelling typically requires a password, reflecting themes of secrecy and the guarded nature of esoteric knowledge.

Baba Yaga herself is typically portrayed as a hag with bony legs and sharp, iron teeth. Despite her frightening appearance, she is not always a malevolent figure; her character is complex, capable of cruelty as well as generosity—depending on the moral character or the cleverness of the protagonist. This variability in her nature reflects the unpredictability of the natural world she represents and the ambivalence of traditional views toward the elderly and the wise, who are both revered and feared.

In many tales, Baba Yaga's role is pivotal in the hero's quest. She often presents challenges or poses riddles and sets seemingly impossible tasks. Success in these tasks typically requires not only bravery and strength but also cunning, respect for the elder's wisdom, and adherence to specific moral codes, such as honor and honesty. This aspect of her character emphasizes the value of wisdom and respect, teaching that supernatural assistance must be earned and that magical creatures like Baba Yaga are not to be trifled with.

One of the most recurrent themes in stories involving Baba Yaga is transformation. She often sends heroes on quests that transform them, pushing them beyond their limits and forcing them to evolve. These quests usually involve retrieving magical objects or rescuing characters who have been transformed or imprisoned. This transformative journey highlights the role of the supernatural as a catalyst for personal growth and change.

Baba Yaga's ambiguity extends to her tools and the objects associated with her. She is often described riding in a mortar, steering with a pestle, and sweeping away her tracks with a broom, tools that link her to the themes of death and regeneration. The mortar and pestle, tools used to grind and mix substances, symbolize the blending of magical ingredients, while the broom represents the traditional female role of the caretaker who controls domestic space, yet here it is subverted to cover tracks and hide intentions.

In a broader cultural context, Baba Yaga can be seen as a guardian of the frontier between the known and the unknown, civilization and the wild, life and death. She challenges the idea of binary opposites, embodying instead a spectrum of possibilities and serving as a reminder that nature and the supernatural are not merely benevolent or malevolent but a combination of both.

Vampires - The Evolution of a Mythological Archetype

The figure of the vampire has haunted the human imagination across cultures and centuries, evolving from folkloric roots into a complex symbol in modern mythology and popular culture. This evolution reflects a rich tapestry of beliefs about death, the afterlife, morality, and the nature of evil. The vampire myth has served various social and psychological functions, providing a means to explore human fears and desires.

The concept of the vampire emerged independently in various cultures, with early forms appearing in ancient civilizations such as Egypt and Greece. However, the vampire as commonly understood today is largely a product of Eastern European folklore, particularly from regions like Serbia, Romania, and Hungary. In these traditions, vampires were often revenants, returning from the dead to harm the living, either by spreading disease or by directly consuming their blood.

These early myths usually attributed vampirism to individuals who had lived wicked lives or who had died in sin. Unnatural deaths, such as suicide or violent death, were also linked to posthumous vampirism. The methods for identifying and dealing with suspected vampires were steeped in local superstition and included practices such as staking through the heart, decapitation, and burning the body.

The transformation of the vampire from a folkloric entity into a dominant figure in literature and film began in the 18th century as Western Europe became fascinated with Eastern European traditions. The publication of the poem "The Vampire" by Heinrich August Ossenfelder in 1748, and later works like John Polidori's "The Vampyre" (1819), which introduced the vampire as a charismatic aristocrat, marked significant shifts in the portrayal of vampires.

However, it was Bram Stoker's "Dracula" (1897) that cemented the image of the vampire in the modern imagination. Stoker's Count Dracula combined aspects of Eastern European folklore with the refined, seductive villain, creating a complex antagonist who was both repulsive and compelling. Dracula's characterization tapped into Victorian fears and fascinations regarding sexuality, exoticism, and disease—themes that continue to be associated with vampires.

Psychologically, vampires can be seen as manifestations of various human fears—fear of the unknown, fear of death, and fear of the outsider. The act of bloodsucking has been interpreted as a metaphor for different forms of exploitation, whether sexual, economic, or social. The vampire's immortality reflects both a human desire for eternal life and the fear of what such a life might entail in terms of loneliness and existential stasis.

Symbolically, vampires often represent the darker aspects of human nature, particularly those that society seeks to suppress or control. Their association with the night and darkness links them to the unconscious mind, where repressed desires lie. The transformative bite of the vampire can also symbolize profound changes in one's identity or beliefs, often carrying connotations of corruption or loss of innocence.

In contemporary media, vampires have diversified significantly, often challenging the traditional boundaries of the genre. Series like Anne Rice's "The Vampire Chronicles" and television shows like "Buffy the Vampire Slayer" have explored the vampire as a more sympathetic and complex character, sometimes struggling with moral and existential dilemmas.

Poludnica: The Noon Witch

Poludnica, known as the Noon Witch or Lady Midday, is a formidable figure associated with the dangers of the midday sun during the harvest season. This mythological entity embodies the natural hazards that agricultural workers faced and serves as a cautionary tale about the importance of rest and the risks of overexertion. Poludnica's story is deeply entwined with the agrarian lifestyle of the Slavic peoples, reflecting their relationship with the rhythms of nature and the challenges of their environment.

Poludnica is often depicted as a tall, ghostly woman dressed in white, or sometimes as an old hag or a beautiful maiden, depending on the region and the tale. She is said to appear in the fields at noon, when the sun is at its highest and most fierce. The timing of her appearances coincides with the time of day when the heat is most oppressive, posing a severe risk of heatstroke to those working in the fields.

The folklore surrounding Poludnica likely originated as an anthropomorphic representation of heatstroke itself. Descriptions of her approach include whispering noises or mirage-like visions, symptoms that also describe the disorientation associated with severe dehydration and sun exposure. She is said to engage with laborers, asking difficult questions or engaging them in conversation. Should they answer incorrectly or not pay her the respect she demands, she strikes them down with illness or madness.

The myth of Poludnica served several functional purposes in Slavic villages. Primarily, it functioned as a health advisory, personifying the dangerous heat of the noon sun to warn agricultural workers to take shelter during the hottest part of the day, thus avoiding heatstroke. The personification of this threat in the form of Poludnica added a narrative element to the precaution, making the danger more vivid and memorable, especially in a largely oral culture.

Moreover, Poludnica's appearances were not only warnings about physical health but also carried moral and social implications. She was a figure that reinforced the importance of proper behavior and respect for the forces of nature, which could be as nurturing as they were destructive. Her interactions with the peasants underscored the necessity of humility, caution, and preparedness.

Symbolically, Poludnica encapsulates the hardships of peasant life and the ever-present risks inherent in subsistence farming. Her dual nature as both beautiful and terrifying can be seen as a reflection of nature itself, which is both the source of life and a constant threat. In this capacity, Poludnica is akin to other mythological figures that symbolize natural dualities and the fine line between nourishment and destruction.

Protective Charms and Rituals in Slavic Tradition

In Slavic tradition, a rich array of protective charms and rituals permeates the cultural and spiritual life of the community. These practices, rooted in a worldview where the spiritual realm is closely intertwined with the physical, serve to safeguard individuals, families, and communities from misfortune, illness, and malevolent forces.

Slavic protective rituals and charms are deeply connected to the agrarian calendar, the natural landscape, and the family unit. They often involve the use of sacred objects, herbal concoctions, and specific incantations that are believed to possess the power to avert harm and attract good fortune. These practices are not only about warding off evil but also about maintaining balance and harmony within the individual and the community.

One of the central aspects of Slavic protective practices involves safeguarding the home, which is seen as a sanctuary but also a vulnerable point where evil forces might enter. The Domovoi, a household spirit revered across Slavic cultures, plays a key role in these practices. Families would often leave offerings of bread, salt, or milk to appease this spirit, hoping to ensure peace and prosperity within their homes. Rituals to protect the home might also involve hanging garlic or herbs, such as mugwort and St. John's wort, over doors and windows to ward off evil spirits.

Agriculture being a cornerstone of life, many Slavic rituals focus on protecting crops and livestock. During important agricultural milestones, such as planting or harvesting, rituals are performed to ensure a bountiful yield and protect against natural calamities. One common practice is the blessing of fields with holy water or the scattering of consecrated poppy seeds to promote fertility and protection. Livestock, too, are often the focus of protective rituals; animals might be adorned with red ribbons or bells to ward off evil spirits.

Personal protection in Slavic tradition frequently involves amulets or talismans. These objects, often crafted from natural materials such as wood, stone, or bones, are typically worn on the body or placed in personal belongings. Symbols such as the thunder mark (a symbol of the god Perun), the sun, and the tree of life are commonly featured on these amulets, each invoking different aspects of protection and blessing. Amulets are often consecrated through rituals involving prayers, incantations, and sometimes the involvement of a village elder or a shaman.

Life's transitions are particularly vulnerable times, necessitating specific protective rituals. Birth, marriage, and death are all heavily ritualized, with various customs designed to safeguard the participants and ensure favorable outcomes. For example, newborns might be given a small bracelet made of amber to protect against the evil eye, while weddings might involve circling a fire to purify and protect the newlyweds. Funerary rituals, rich with protective symbolism, are designed to secure a safe passage for the deceased's soul into the afterlife.

Slavic festivals and seasonal rites also incorporate elements of protection, linking the community's well-being with the cycles of nature. Kupala Night, celebrated on the summer solstice, includes jumping over fires to cleanse from sin and bad luck and bathing in rivers to gain health and protection. Similarly, during Maslenitsa, the celebration marking the end of winter, effigies symbolizing winter are burnt to cleanse the community of the past year's hardships and negative energies.

Spirits and Demons in African Folklore

African folklore is a vast, intricate web of stories, beliefs, and characters that vary widely across the continent's many cultures. Central to these narratives are the spirits and demons that interact with the human world in profound and often moralistic ways. These entities are are deeply embedded in the cosmology and daily life of the people, reflecting their intrinsic values, fears, and the mysteries of the natural world around them.

The Concept of Good vs. Evil in African Mythology

The dichotomy of good versus evil is a central theme in mythologies worldwide, and African mythology is no exception. However, African mythological narratives often present these concepts within a framework that emphasizes balance, community, and the interconnectedness of all things, rather than as a straightforward battle between opposing forces. This chapter explores how various African cultures conceptualize good and evil, highlighting the complexity and diversity of these traditions.

African mythology is as diverse as the continent itself, encompassing a wide range of beliefs from hundreds of different cultures. Each tradition offers its own interpretations of good and evil, often influenced by local customs, social structures, and natural environments. Despite this diversity, several common themes emerge, including the importance of balance, the moral responsibilities of individuals to their community, and the belief that evil often arises from social discord or spiritual imbalance.

Many African mythologies do not view good and evil as absolute states but rather as complementary forces that must be kept in balance to ensure harmony and health in the world. For example, in the cosmology of the Yoruba of Nigeria, the universe is governed by a pantheon of deities known as Orishas, who represent various natural and moral forces. Among these is Eshu, the trickster god, who embodies both chaos and order, serving as a mediator and a messenger between humans and the other Orishas. Eshu's actions can lead to trouble or fortune, reminding followers of the need for wisdom and vigilance in their moral choices.

African myths frequently use stories of conflict and resolution to teach moral lessons. These stories often feature heroes who must undergo trials, make sacrifices, or use their wisdom to restore balance to their communities. In these narratives, evil is rarely an external force to be defeated but is often a consequence of personal failings like greed, pride, or disrespect for communal norms.

One prominent example can be found in the stories of Anansi, the spider figure common to Akan folklore in Ghana. Anansi is a complex character who can be cunning, selfish, and disruptive. His adventures often result in troubles that reflect his moral weaknesses. Yet, Anansi is also a culture hero who brings knowledge and benefits to people, showcasing the dual nature of his actions and underscoring the nuanced view of morality prevalent in many African stories.

In African mythology, the well-being of the community often takes precedence over individual desires. Many myths emphasize that evil results from actions that disturb social harmony or breach communal laws. For instance, among the Igbo of Nigeria, the Earth goddess, Ala, is central to enforcing moral law. Violations against her laws are considered both moral and spiritual failings that bring about chaos and suffering in the form of poor harvests, sickness, or social strife. Here, evil is understood as anything that disrupts the health and stability of the community, and good is that which promotes social cohesion and prosperity.

Eshu: The Divine Messenger of Yoruba Mythology

Eshu, also known as Elegba or Exu in some traditions, is one of the most complex deities in Yoruba mythology. Known primarily as the trickster god and the deity of crossroads, Eshu plays a crucial role in the Yoruba pantheon as the communicator between the divine and the human, the enforcer of fate, and the god of chance and chaos. His dualistic nature makes him a figure of both reverence and caution within the Yoruba culture and beyond.

In Yoruba belief, Eshu is often depicted as a mediator who possesses the power to influence fortune. As the god of crossroads, he represents decision-making and the inherent uncertainty in choices. Unlike Western interpretations of trickster figures who may solely embody deceit, Eshu embodies both the positive and negative outcomes of trickery, symbolizing the unpredictable nature of life.

Eshu is also portrayed wearing a hat split down the middle, half red and half black, symbolizing his dual nature. He carries a club with which he can stir up trouble as easily as he can provide wise guidance. His iconography often includes carved figures with phallic symbols, emphasizing fertility and the creative (and sometimes chaotic) power of nature.

Numerous myths highlight Eshu's role in both creating trouble and delivering justice. One popular tale describes how Eshu once walked between two friends wearing his two-colored hat, visible only on one side. Upon his departure, the friends quarreled over the color of the hat, nearly leading to blows before Eshu revealed himself, teaching them a lesson on perspective and the ease of misunderstanding and conflict.

Another significant aspect of Eshu's mythology involves his interaction with Ifá, the divination system used by the Yoruba. Eshu is essential to Ifá for he delivers the sacrifices to the other gods and ensures the messages of the oracle are accurate. His role here is not merely as a trickster but as a guardian of truth, highlighting the dual aspect of his nature as both a potential source of discord and a crucial agent of balance and righteousness.

Eshu is one of the Orishas who must be honored during any ceremony before any other gods, due to his role as the opener of the way. Without acknowledging Eshu, it is believed that prayers will not reach the other deities, and chaos may ensue. Offerings to Eshu typically include palm oil, small rats, fish, and corncakes, and they are left at crossroads, markets, and other liminal spaces that he governs.

In Yoruba culture, Eshu is also considered the protector of travelers and is thought to ward off misfortune for those who respect him or invoke his name. His followers wear charms and amulets known as "Eshu Laroye" which are believed to protect them from the trickery of others and to ensure safe passage through literal and metaphorical crossroads.

Eshu exemplifies the Yoruba understanding of the world as a place of complexity, where good and evil are not always distinct and where the truth depends on perspective. His capacity to teach through trickery and to reveal deeper truths through chaos places him as a central figure in conveying moral and ethical teachings within the Yoruba community.

Tokoloshe: The Malevolent Spirit

This mischievous and malevolent spirit is a staple of the folklore of the Zulu and Xhosa people of Southern Africa. Often described as a dwarf-like water sprite, the Tokoloshe is feared for its supernatural abilities to cause harm and mischief to humans. Understanding the Tokoloshe provides valuable insights into the cultural and spiritual life of Southern African communities, reflecting their beliefs about the supernatural and its influence on the material world.

The Tokoloshe is traditionally described as a small, hairy creature, somewhat akin to a gremlin or goblin in Western folklore. It is said to be created from a corpse through witchcraft, serving sorcerers and witches as an agent to torment those who cross them. The creature is known for its ghastly appearance, often characterized by its gouged-out eyes and gaunt, animal-like features. Despite its small stature, the Tokoloshe is endowed with great strength and stealth, making it a fearsome entity in the folklore of the region.

According to traditional beliefs, the Tokoloshe can become invisible by drinking water and can induce illness, death, or general misfortune to those it targets. Families who believe themselves to be at risk of Tokoloshe visitation might take precautions such as placing bricks beneath the legs of their beds to raise them higher off the ground. This practice is thought to protect sleepers by making it difficult for the Tokoloshe, who is reputed to be fond of creeping upon sleeping victims, to reach them.

The lore surrounding the Tokoloshe is also linked to societal taboos and norms. It often serves as a cautionary figure to reinforce moral behavior. In some tales, the Tokoloshe is a punisher of the wicked or those who have strayed from the ethical path expected by the community.

In this way, the Tokoloshe's malevolence is not random but targeted at those deemed deserving of punishment.

The Tokoloshe myth can be seen as a reflection of the social and psychological anxieties of the communities that believe in it. Anthropologists and cultural scholars often interpret the Tokoloshe as embodying the collective fears of evil, misfortune, and the unknown. The ritual precautions taken against the Tokoloshe help to provide a sense of control over these fears, offering psychological comfort through the performance of protective traditions.

Moreover, the belief in the Tokoloshe underscores the importance of respecting the supernatural elements that are perceived to permeate the natural world. This respect is central to maintaining harmony within the community and the environment. Disrespecting these forces, whether through moral failures or breaking taboos, is thought to invite chaos and disaster, as personified by the Tokoloshe.

In contemporary Southern Africa, the Tokoloshe continues to be a potent part of cultural expression, although perceptions have evolved over time. While some people continue to hold genuine fear of the Tokoloshe, in urban areas and among younger generations, the creature is often viewed more symbolically or with a degree of skepticism. Modern media and literature sometimes employ the Tokoloshe in a more figurative manner, using it as a metaphor for human evils or social issues.

Mami Wata: The Water Spirit

Mami Wata, a name that translates to "Mother Water," is a pervasive figure in African mythology, revered and feared across numerous African cultures and among the African diaspora. This water spirit embodies a complex blend of attributes, from beauty and seduction to healing and protective powers, often associated with water bodies such as rivers, lakes, and the ocean.

Mami Wata is often depicted as a mermaid-like figure with a human upper body and the lower body of a fish or serpent. This imagery is not indigenous to Africa alone but shows influences from European, Middle Eastern, and Indian depictions of similar water deities, reflecting the historical interactions between Africa and other regions through trade, colonization, and the spread of religions.

The syncretism in Mami Wata's portrayal highlights her role as a bridge between various cultural elements and traditions. She is sometimes depicted holding large pythons, which are sacred in many West African cultures, or adorned with modern symbols of wealth and exoticism like mirrors, combs, and watches, suggesting her connection to commerce and the material wealth brought by overseas traders.

Mami Wata is attributed with a dual nature; she can bestow wealth, beauty, and healing, but she is also capable of abduction and destruction, reflecting the unpredictable nature of water. Her followers believe that encounters with Mami Wata can lead to spiritual transformation, often marked by a period of illness or disappearance from the community, followed by a return with newfound wealth or healing abilities.

Worship practices dedicated to Mami Wata involve elaborate rituals that include music, dancing, and the offering of gifts such as clothing, jewelry, and perfumes to appease the spirit and seek her blessings. These rituals are often colorful and festive but also carry an undercurrent of fear and respect for her formidable powers.

Mami Wata is a symbol of fertility and sexuality, connected to the life-giving properties of water. Her association with fertility is not just about procreation but also encompasses economic and spiritual abundance. However, her connection to the depths of the ocean also links her to the subconscious and the unknown, making her a figure of mystery and depth.

She is also seen as a guardian of nature and is believed to protect the waters she inhabits, reflecting indigenous conservation practices that recognize the dependency of human life on the natural environment. In this role, Mami Wata serves as a reminder of the need to maintain ecological balance and respect for natural resources.

In modern times, Mami Wata remains a powerful cultural icon in Africa and among African communities worldwide. She appears in contemporary arts, literature, and film, often used to explore themes of identity, diaspora, and environmentalism.

Ancestral Spirits and Witchcraft in African Mythology

In African mythology, ancestral spirits and witchcraft play critical and complex roles, deeply woven into the social, spiritual, and moral fabric of various cultures across the continent. These elements are pivotal in understanding how communities relate to the spiritual realm, navigate daily life, and interpret the forces that influence their world.

Ancestral Spirits: Guardians and Guides

Ancestral spirits, or the spirits of departed family members, are revered across many African cultures. These spirits are believed to act as intermediaries between the living and the spiritual realm, playing a protective role and offering guidance to their living relatives. The veneration of ancestors is rooted in the belief that the dead have a continued existence and remain interested in the affairs of the world they left behind.

In societies such as those of the Akan in Ghana, the Zulu in South Africa, and the Yoruba in Nigeria, ancestors are actively incorporated into daily life through rituals, prayers, and offerings. These practices are not mere acts of remembrance but are vital to maintaining the balance and harmony of the community. Ancestors are often consulted through divination during important decisions or life events such as births, marriages, and funerals, reflecting their integral role in the social and moral order of the community.

Ancestral spirits are believed to provide protection, prosperity, and health to their descendants. They are also seen as upholders of moral values and traditional customs, punishing those who stray from the path of righteousness or who fail to respect cultural norms. This disciplinary aspect underscores the ancestors' role in social regulation, ensuring that ethical behaviors are maintained across generations.

However, if neglected or angered, ancestral spirits can also bring misfortune, illness, or general unrest to individuals or the community. This belief underscores the reciprocal relationship between the living and the dead, where respect and proper rituals must be observed to maintain favor and balance.

Witchcraft: Power and Ambiguity

Witchcraft in African mythology often carries a dual connotation, associated with both protective and malevolent powers. It involves the practice of magical skills, spells, and the invocation of spirits in ways that can either harm or heal, depending on the intent of the practitioner.

In many communities, witchcraft is feared due to its association with sorcery and the infliction of harm through supernatural means. Accusations of witchcraft can lead to social ostracism or worse, reflecting deep-seated fears and the potential for witchcraft to disrupt community harmony.

However, witchcraft can also be viewed positively, seen in the figure of the traditional healer or witch doctor, who uses knowledge of herbs, spirits, and rituals to cure illnesses, protect against evil, and counteract harmful spells. This aspect of witchcraft highlights its role in health and well-being, serving as a critical component of the community's medical and spiritual life.

The beliefs in ancestral spirits and witchcraft carry significant implications. They reinforce communal values by linking individuals' actions to the welfare of the broader community, both living and ancestral. These beliefs foster a sense of continuity and collective responsibility, ensuring that cultural practices and moral standards are passed down through generations.

Protective Measures Against Dark Forces in African Traditions

In African traditions, the spiritual realm is intricately woven into the fabric of daily life, influencing health, prosperity, and community well-being. Protective measures against dark forces form an essential aspect of these traditions, reflecting a deep understanding of the spiritual landscape and its impact on the physical world.

In many African cultures, dark forces are often perceived as malevolent spirits, ancestors who have been wronged, or entities created through witchcraft intended to cause harm. These forces can affect every aspect of life, from personal health to agricultural productivity and community harmony. Protection against such forces is therefore seen as vital for survival and prosperity.

One of the primary methods of protection involves community rituals and ceremonies that cleanse and fortify the spiritual environment. These ceremonies might include dances, chants, and the use of drums to invoke protective spirits or ancestors and drive away harmful entities. An example is the Zulu practice of 'ukuphahla,' where offerings and prayers are made to the ancestors, asking for their protection and guidance.

In many West African traditions, annual festivals serve both to celebrate the community and to renew its collective spiritual protection. During these festivals, rituals are performed to reinforce the barriers between the human world and the realm of dark spirits, ensuring that malevolent forces do not cross into the community.

Use of Amulets and Talismans

Amulets and talismans are widespread in African protective practices. These objects, often made from herbs, minerals, animal parts, or sacred objects, are believed to carry intrinsic protective powers. They are commonly worn on the body or placed in homes and fields to ward off evil spirits and negative energies.

In the Horn of Africa, for instance, the 'Evil Eye' is a prevalent concern, with amulets often used to protect against the misfortune it is believed to cause. Similarly, in parts of West Africa, protective charms might be prepared by traditional healers or 'witch doctors' who imbue them with spiritual significance through prayers and rituals.

Herbal Medicines and Spiritual Baths

Herbal medicines and spiritual baths play crucial roles in protection against dark forces. These practices are often overseen by traditional healers who possess knowledge of the spiritual properties of plants and minerals. In South Africa, for example, the practice of 'smudging' involves burning specific herbs to cleanse a space or person of evil spirits or bad luck.

Spiritual baths often incorporate a mixture of sacred water and herbs and are used to wash away malevolent influences. These baths are sometimes accompanied by incantations or prayers that increase their efficacy and tailor their protective properties to the needs of an individual or community.

Divination and Spiritual Consultation

Divination is a critical aspect of identifying and counteracting dark forces within many African cultures. Through various forms of divination, healers or diviners can diagnose spiritual problems, identify the sources of malevolent magic, and recommend solutions to protect or cleanse the affected individuals or areas.

Divination methods vary widely but often involve the interpretation of the patterns formed by throwing bones, stones, or shells. The diviner interprets these patterns to receive messages from the ancestors or other spiritual entities about the nature of the problem and the necessary protective measures.

Demonic Figures of Chinese Mythology

Chinese mythology, with its rich pantheon of gods, heroes, and mystical beings, also features a variety of demonic figures. These entities often serve as antagonists in mythological stories, representing natural disasters, moral lessons, or challenges to be overcome by heroes or deities. Unlike the stark evil depicted in Western demonology, Chinese demonic figures can have nuanced roles, ranging from malevolent to mischievous, and are deeply woven into the cultural and spiritual fabric of Chinese folklore.

Baigujing: Deception and Morality in "Journey to the West"

Baigujing, a lesser-known but pivotal character in the classic Chinese novel "Journey to the West," embodies themes of deception, transformation, and moral testing. This white bone spirit is a demoness known for her ability to shape-shift and her cunning attempts to disrupt the pilgrimage of the monk Xuanzang and his protectors.

"Journey to the West," written by Wu Cheng'en in the 16th century, is one of the Four Great Classical Novels of Chinese literature. The narrative details the adventures of the Buddhist monk Xuanzang as he travels to India to obtain sacred texts, accompanied by his protectors, including the mischievous and powerful Monkey King, Sun Wukong. Baigujing appears in a segment of the journey, presenting a significant challenge to the group through her deceptions.

Baigujing is introduced as a demon with a propensity for consuming human flesh, particularly that of holy men, which she believes will grant her immortality. Her name, translating to "White Bone Spirit," reflects her ability to strip down to her skeletal form, which she uses to disguise herself and manipulate others. Throughout her encounters with Xuanzang's party, Baigujing demonstrates a deep understanding of human psychology and spiritual vulnerabilities, using these insights to craft her illusions.

Baigujing's primary tactic against Xuanzang and his companions is transformation. She takes on multiple guises, including those of a young woman, an old man, and a child, each designed to evoke sympathy or moral obligation from the travelers. Her transformations are not merely physical but are accompanied by crafted stories that play on the virtues and vices of her targets, particularly Xuanzang's compassion and the protective instincts of his disciples.

Her most notable attempt involves posing as a filial girl mourning her deceased parents, hoping to trick Xuanzang into giving her a Buddhist funeral recitation, which she plans to use to her advantage. Each of her disguises is crafted to test the resolve, wisdom, and spiritual insight of the pilgrims, making her one of the most psychologically complex antagonists in the novel.

The confrontations between Baigujing and Sun Wukong form the climax of her narrative arc. Sun Wukong, with his ability to see through demonic deceptions, repeatedly unmasks Baigujing, yet struggles to convince the naive Xuanzang of her true nature. These episodes highlight a recurring motif in "Journey to the West" — the tension between appearance and reality and the challenge of discerning truth in a world replete with illusions.

Baigujing's eventual defeat by Sun Wukong, who must use a combination of brute force and cleverness, underscores the novel's deeper philosophical and moral lessons: that spiritual discernment is crucial and that maintaining one's moral and spiritual integrity requires vigilance and wisdom.

Baigujing serves as a symbol of the external and internal challenges faced by individuals on the spiritual path. Her ability to exploit the virtues of the pilgrims, particularly Xuanzang's compassion, illustrates the complexity of moral and spiritual life; virtues can become vulnerabilities when not tempered with wisdom and discernment.

Baigujing's story conveys the idea that evil is persistent and adaptive, often cloaked in the guise of innocence or righteousness. The repetitive nature of her confrontations with the pilgrims reflects the ongoing nature of spiritual tests and the necessity of constant vigilance on the path to enlightenment.

Nian: The Mythical Beast of Chinese New Year

The legend of Nian is an integral part of Chinese folklore, particularly associated with the celebration of the Lunar New Year. The myth of this fearsome beast not only explains the origins of various New Year traditions but also encapsulates the themes of renewal, community protection, and the triumph over evil that are central to the festival.

Nian, whose name means "year" in Chinese, is traditionally depicted as a large, ferocious beast with sharp teeth and horns. According to legend, Nian would emerge from its hiding place in the mountains or under the sea once a year to terrorize villages, devouring crops, livestock, and even villagers, particularly children. The annual arrival of Nian instilled fear and prompted ancient communities to seek ways to protect themselves and ward off the beast.

The story of Nian is thought to have originated from ancient agricultural societies that battled against natural predators and harsh environments. Over time, the legend evolved from a simple tale of a monster attack to a more complex narrative encompassing themes of harm and protection, good fortune, and the start of a new year. As with many myths, the tale of Nian was likely influenced by real events, such as wild animal attacks or natural disasters, which were mythologized over generations.

The practices associated with the Lunar New Year, such as the use of fireworks, red decorations, and loud drumming, are deeply rooted in the legend of Nian. It is said that the villagers discovered that loud noises, bright lights, and the color red were particularly effective in scaring the beast away. These elements were incorporated into the annual celebration to ensure Nian would not return, symbolizing the community's resilience and collective effort to protect itself from external threats.

Fireworks and firecrackers, now ubiquitous during Chinese New Year celebrations, reflect the original use of loud bangs to frighten Nian. The use of red, seen in lanterns, scrolls, and clothing, has transcended its original protective purpose to symbolize luck and prosperity. Additionally, the lion dance, another highlight of New Year festivities, is performed to drive away evil spirits and bring good luck, echoing the ancient rituals performed to scare off Nian.

In modern times, the legend of Nian continues to be a focal point of Lunar New Year celebrations, serving as a reminder of the historical and cultural origins of these practices. The story is also used as a teaching tool, conveying messages about courage, community, and the importance of safeguarding one's home and loved ones from misfortune.

The myth of Nian is incorporated into school curricula around the time of the Lunar New Year to teach children about cultural heritage and traditional values. It also serves as an example of how ancient societies interpreted and conceptualized natural phenomena and dangers through storytelling, imbuing these stories with moral and practical lessons.

Xiezhi: The Emblem of Justice

The Xiezhi, a mythical creature from Chinese mythology, embodies the principles of justice and lawfulness. This legendary creature, often depicted as a goat-like beast with a single horn, has been a potent symbol in Chinese culture, particularly within the judicial system. The Xiezhi's ability to discern truth from falsehood and its role in promoting righteous behavior make it a fascinating subject within the broader context of mythical symbols of justice.

The Xiezhi is first mentioned in ancient Chinese texts as a creature capable of discerning guilt. It is said to have the power to strike down wrongdoers and is often depicted in art as attacking or eating those found guilty of crimes. Its physical appearance, sometimes described akin to a goat or unicorn, symbolizes its purity and the singularity of its purpose. This creature combines elements of strength and discernment, making it a unique figure in the pantheon of mythical beasts.

In ancient Chinese lore, the Xiezhi's most notable attribute is its connection to legalism and justice. The creature is said to have been used by legendary judges and kings as a symbol of their commitment to justice and their ability to enforce it. The Xiezhi could supposedly point its horn at the guilty party in a dispute, thus resolving legal matters without error. This mythological attribute highlights the cultural value placed on fairness and the ideal of an infallible justice system.

Over time, the Xiezhi became a symbol commonly used in the robes and accessories of judges and officials during the imperial eras. Its image was embroidered on judicial robes and featured in courtrooms and legal documents as an emblem of impartial judgment and the moral rectitude expected of those who enforce the law.

The representation of the Xiezhi in Chinese art has evolved through dynasties but consistently reflects themes of justice and moral authority. Statues and reliefs of the Xiezhi can be found in ancient temples and palaces, symbolizing the protective and judicial role of the structure's inhabitants. In paintings and literature, the Xiezhi is often depicted in scenes involving judicial proceedings or as part of a narrative illustrating moral principles.

In contemporary China, the Xiezhi remains a cultural symbol associated with justice and law. It appears in modern artworks, legal texts, and as a mascot in various legal institutions, serving as a bridge between ancient judicial practices and modern legal values. The creature's enduring presence in the judicial realm underscores its significance as a symbol of unwavering justice and the cultural continuity of legal ideals.

Jiangshi: The Hopping Vampire

The Jiangshi, often referred to in Western contexts as the "Chinese hopping vampire" or "hopping zombie," is a mythical creature that embodies unique aspects of Chinese views on death and the supernatural. Unlike the Western vampire, which is typically seen as a bloodsucking fiend, the Jiangshi blends elements of vampires and zombies, reflecting traditional Chinese beliefs about the spirit and the body after death.

The myth of the Jiangshi is thought to have originated during the Qing dynasty, though elements of the legend can be traced back earlier. The term "Jiangshi" translates to "stiff corpse," a reference to the creature's rigid movements, often depicted as hopping with its arms outstretched due to rigor mortis. This imagery stems from the belief that certain corpses, if improperly handled or if they died under unfortunate or supernatural circumstances, could reanimate and return to their homes by hopping.

Jiangshi are typically described as wearing Qing dynasty funeral attire, which reinforces their connection to death and the afterlife. Their appearance is often grotesque, with a pale complexion and sometimes decayed features, similar to that of a zombie. However, unlike Western zombies, Jiangshi are driven by their need to absorb life essence (qi) from the living, rather than to consume flesh. This need arises from the traditional Chinese belief in the vital energy that sustains life, which the Jiangshi lacks.

The legend of the Jiangshi is deeply intertwined with Daoist customs and funeral practices. One popular folk belief is that a Jiangshi arises when a person's soul fails to leave their body due to improper death rituals, suicide, or simply the victim of a violent death. The fear of such reanimation led to specific practices to prevent the dead from becoming Jiangshi, including the use of protective talismans or ensuring that the corpse was buried properly and without delay.

In some tales, the Jiangshi returns to its family home to bring misfortune to its relatives or the community, prompting the need for a Daoist priest to perform rites to reincorporate or pacify the wandering spirit. The involvement of religious specialists highlights the community's role in managing the boundaries between the living and the dead.

In modern times, the Jiangshi has transcended its folkloric roots to become a prominent figure in popular culture, particularly in Hong Kong cinema during the 1980s and 1990s. Films like "Mr. Vampire" and its sequels portrayed Jiangshi with a blend of horror and comedy, contributing to the creature's popularity and its recognition outside China.

Tao Tie: The Gluttonous Beast

The Tao Tie is one of the most enigmatic and ancient symbols found in Chinese mythology, often associated with greed and gluttony. This mythical creature appears prominently in Chinese bronze ware from the Shang and Zhou dynasties, where it is typically depicted as a motif with a ferociously detailed face but no body.

The Tao Tie is thought to originate from totemic symbols used by ancient Chinese clans. Over time, it evolved into a decorative motif that adorned ritual bronze vessels used in ancestral worship and state ceremonies. These bronzes, which include ding vessels and other food containers, suggest a connection between the Tao Tie and themes of consumption and feasting, reflecting its role as a symbol of both nourishment and excess.

The creature's name, "Tao Tie," translates roughly to "gluttonous ogre," which aligns with its depiction in folklore as a creature driven by insatiable hunger. In some interpretations, the Tao Tie is considered one of the "Four Evil Creatures of the World" in ancient Chinese culture, representing the negative consequences of unchecked appetite and desire.

In art, the Tao Tie is often portrayed with a zoomorphic face, combining features of various animals such as dragons, tigers, and rams. It typically has bulging eyes, a wide mouth, and sharp fangs, which are thought to intimidate viewers and ward off evil spirits. The body of the Tao Tie is rarely depicted in full, which some scholars interpret as symbolizing the beast's insatiable nature—without a body, it can never be fully satiated.

The use of the Tao Tie motif on bronze vessels has dual symbolism. While it beautifies these important cultural artifacts, it also serves as a cautionary emblem that admonishes the user to restrain their greed. This aligns with Confucian and Taoist thought, which emphasizes moderation and ethical living.

Though specific myths focusing solely on the Tao Tie are rare, the creature is often mentioned in various texts and myths where it interacts with gods and heroes. In these stories, the Tao Tie's boundless hunger symbolizes the dangers of overindulgence and the moral failures associated with it. For rulers and leaders, the Tao Tie serves as a reminder of the responsibilities they carry and the repercussions of exploiting their power for personal gain.

The Tao Tie's depiction in ancient Chinese culture explores the tension between civilization and barbarism, and between human desires and societal needs. This creature embodies the consequences of losing control over one's appetites, serving as a metaphor for the destructive nature of human desires when left unchecked.

In Confucian thought, the Tao Tie warns against the dangers of excess and the moral decay that can result from greed and selfishness. It encourages leaders to consider their actions' impact on their subjects and to cultivate virtue and moderation in their governance.

Malevolent Entities of Native American Mythology

Native American mythology, encompassing a vast array of tribal nations each with its own rich traditions, stories, and spiritual beliefs, includes a variety of malevolent entities.

Thunderbird vs. Water Panther: Archetypal Conflict

In Native American mythology, few motifs are as pervasive or as symbolically potent as the battle between the Thunderbird and the Water Panther. This archetypal conflict represents not only the clash of elemental forces but also encapsulates deeper cultural and spiritual lessons about balance, power, and morality.

The Thunderbird is a mythical creature revered across numerous Native American cultures. It is often depicted as a massive bird, capable of creating storms and thunder as it flaps its wings. As a being of the air and sky, the Thunderbird symbolizes strength, protection, and purity. It is often considered a guardian spirit that combats evil influences and maintains order in the universe.

In contrast, the Water Panther, or Mishipeshu, features prominently in the myths of the Great Lakes and northeastern woodland tribes. This creature, often depicted as part panther and part aquatic creature with scales and horns, embodies the power of the underwater world. The Water Panther is associated with the darker, unpredictable forces of nature, governing rivers, lakes, and other bodies of water.

The conflict between the Thunderbird and the Water Panther reflects the natural chaos inherent in the world and the necessary balance that must be maintained between contrasting forces. The Thunderbird, with its association with the upper world, and the Water Panther, a creature of the underworld, embody the tension between sky and water, air and earth, order and chaos.

In many stories, the Thunderbird is seen protecting the people from the Water Panther's malevolent disruptions, which often include floods, whirlpools, and other water-related disasters. These tales serve to educate the community about the dangers of the natural world while also instilling a respect for the creatures that inhabit these realms, acknowledging their power and the need for harmony between opposing forces.

The mythological conflict between these two powerful beings holds significant ceremonial and cultural importance. For many tribes, these stories are told as part of ritual practices, particularly in ceremonies that call for protection or blessings from the natural elements. For instance, the Thunderbird is often invoked for rain and fertility of the land, while the Water Panther might be respected and appeased to prevent drowning and to ensure safe travel across waters.

These creatures also appear extensively in tribal art, including totems, petroglyphs, and ceremonial regalia, symbolizing their integral role in tribal identity and spiritual life. The imagery serves not only as a reminder of the myths themselves but also as a symbol of the tribe's respect for the forces these creatures represent. Modern retellings and adaptations of these myths often emphasize the need for an ecological balance and are used in educational contexts to teach both Native American history and environmental stewardship.

Skinwalkers: The Shapeshifters of Navajo

Skinwalkers, known as 'yee naaldlooshii' in the Navajo language, which translates to "he who walks on all fours," are one of the most chilling and taboo aspects of Navajo mythology. As shapeshifters and witches, Skinwalkers occupy a complex role in Navajo culture, encapsulating themes of morality, the supernatural, and cultural taboos.

The concept of the Skinwalker is deeply rooted in Navajo tradition and is part of a larger belief system that includes witchcraft, known as the 'Witchery Way.' According to Navajo lore, Skinwalkers are witches who have learned to transform into the forms of animals by wearing their skins, typically those of predators such as wolves, coyotes, bears, or birds of prey. This ability is considered an ultimate taboo, as it involves violating the cultural laws that govern the use of animal pelts in Navajo society and the natural order.

Skinwalkers are reputed to possess vast supernatural powers, including superhuman strength, the ability to change shape, speed, and agility, and the skills to cast spells and curses. They are most often described in stories as malevolent beings who use their powers for harm, inciting fear and misfortune among communities. Unlike other cultural shapeshifters who may transform for various reasons, Skinwalkers are almost universally associated with evil intentions.

The practice of wearing the skins of animals to transform is particularly transgressive in Navajo culture, where certain animals are considered sacred and their representations are limited to specific uses and contexts. The Skinwalker's violation of these norms through the use of pelts is a symbolic crossing of moral and spiritual boundaries, turning them into pariahs within their communities.

Skinwalkers are not merely mythical creatures; they serve as a cultural warning against the dangers of misusing spiritual power. In Navajo culture, traditional healers and spiritual leaders, known as medicine men and women, use their powers to heal, protect, and guide their communities. The Skinwalker, in contrast, uses similar knowledge for selfish and destructive ends. This dichotomy underscores a fundamental belief within Navajo and many other Indigenous cultures: that spiritual power is a double-edged sword that must be wielded responsibly.

Stories about Skinwalkers are not just old wives' tales but are a part of the living oral tradition that serves to educate and warn community members about the moral and spiritual laws that govern their lives. Accounts of encounters with Skinwalkers are treated with great seriousness in Navajo communities and are often shared privately or hesitantly, reflecting the deep cultural sensitivity and fear surrounding these beings.

The Skinwalker has entered broader American pop culture, often losing its specific cultural context and being portrayed in a variety of ways in films, books, and television shows. This has sometimes led to misunderstandings and misrepresentations of Navajo beliefs and practices. For many Navajos, discussions about Skinwalkers with outsiders are avoided, not only because they are considered dangerous but also to prevent the commercialization and trivialization of their culture.

Wendigo: The Spirit of Winter and Starvation

The Wendigo is a powerful and terrifying figure in the folklore of several Algonquian-speaking peoples in North America, including the Ojibwe, Saulteaux, Cree, Naskapi, and Innu. This mythical creature or spirit, associated with the cold, hunger, and the harshness of winter, embodies the fear of both the physical environment and the potential for humans to succumb to their darkest urges.

The Wendigo legend originates from the cultural traditions of various tribes in the regions surrounding the Great Lakes of Canada and the northern United States. The creature is often described as gaunt to the point of emaciation, reflecting its association with starvation and insatiable hunger. Its eyes are said to be pushed back deep into their sockets, and it has tattered lips from constant hunger. The Wendigo's heart, according to some tales, is made of ice. Its overall appearance and demeanor represent the embodiment of winter's cruelty.

Traditionally, the Wendigo is not only a creature but a symbol of excess and taboo. The most common tale associated with the Wendigo is that of a person who, driven by extreme hunger, resorts to cannibalism and becomes a Wendigo as a result. Thus, the Wendigo myth serves as a moral tale that warns against such taboos as cannibalism, which is viewed among these communities as one of the worst crimes a person can commit, and a symbol of the destructive power of greed and excess.

One of the Wendigo's defining characteristics is its insatiable hunger. The more it eats, the hungrier it becomes; therefore, it grows progressively larger with each victim it devours, so it can never be sated. This aspect of the Wendigo myth speaks to deeper human fears about insatiability and the idea that surrendering to greed or selfishness can lead to a never-ending cycle of destruction. This endless hunger mirrors natural phenomena such as harsh winters, which can seem endlessly bleak and deadly.

The Wendigo serves multiple functions within the storytelling traditions of Native American cultures. Psychologically, it embodies the concept of "Wendigo psychosis," a term that was used historically by anthropologists to describe a condition in which individuals might develop an excessive craving for human flesh. More broadly, the Wendigo represents a cautionary tale about the loss of humanity and the consequences of breaking moral and cultural taboos.

Culturally, the Wendigo is used as a teaching tool. It is a reminder of the balance that must be maintained between individuals and their community, particularly in the sharing of resources during times of scarcity. The Wendigo warns of what can happen when this balance is disrupted, serving as a stark reminder of the importance of community welfare over individual survival.

Dzunukwa: The Wild Woman of the Woods

Dzunukwa, also known as Tsonoqua, Dzonoqua, or the Wild Woman of the Woods, is a central figure in the mythology of the Kwakwaka'wakw people, a First Nations group from the Pacific Northwest region of Canada.

Dzunukwa is often depicted as a giantess with blackened or dark features, bushy hair, and pronounced supernatural attributes. Her most distinctive characteristics include her pursed lips—used to emit a distinctive "huu huu" sound—and her eyes, which are said to be capable of seeing long distances. Descriptions of her appearance and behavior convey a creature that is both formidable and somewhat clumsy, adding a complex layer to her interactions with humans.

In Kwakwaka'wakw culture, Dzunukwa is considered a symbol of wealth and abundance, despite her more ominous reputation as a child-snatcher and a giant of the forest. She is known to carry a large basket on her back, in which she puts children she has captured. However, the children often outsmart her and escape, reflecting common themes in folklore where youth and cunning overcome brute strength and terror.

Her association with wealth is particularly emphasized during potlatch ceremonies, where Dzunukwa masks and dances are performed to recount her stories and symbolize the transfer of wealth. These performances are not only a display of cultural heritage but also a means to pass on moral and practical lessons within the community.

Dzunukwa's role extends beyond the mythical narratives into the very fabric of Kwakwaka'wakw ceremonial life. She is a popular subject in the art and totem poles of the Pacific Northwest, her image serving as a guardian of the people and a reminder of the abundance that the forest holds. Masks representing Dzunukwa are considered powerful spiritual objects and are used in various rituals, including initiation rites and the potlatch, a ceremonial feast with deep social and economic significance.

During these ceremonies, the Dzunukwa mask is worn by dancers who emulate her movements and sounds, bringing her character to life. These performances serve to educate the audience about Dzunukwa's dual nature—her ability to bestow wealth and her potential for destruction—highlighting the balance that individuals must navigate in their own lives.

The stories and depictions of Dzunukwa are imbued with educational purposes, teaching children about the dangers of wandering alone in the woods and the importance of community vigilance. Her narratives often contain elements of caution about the natural world and the boundaries between the human communities and the wild.

Dzunukwa teaches about the value of resourcefulness and bravery. The tales where children escape her grasp are not only thrilling adventures but also parables on the use of wit and courage in the face of danger, and the triumph of the human spirit over overwhelming odds.

Piasa: The Mysterious Bird

The Piasa, or the Piasa Bird, is a creature of Native American folklore, particularly associated with the Illiniwek or Illinois Confederation tribes along the Mississippi River. The Piasa Bird is depicted as a fearsome amalgamation of various animals, with features often including scales, the antlers of a deer, the body of a serpent, and the face of a man. This mythical creature is steeped in mystery and is a prominent figure in the folklore of the region, symbolizing both terror and protection.

The Piasa Bird was first documented by European explorers in the 1670s when Father Jacques Marquette, upon navigating the Mississippi River, recorded seeing a large painting of the creature on the bluffs near present-day Alton, Illinois. Marquette's descriptions, coupled with later accounts by explorers in the same area, depict the Piasa as a large, dragon-like creature painted high on the cliffs, overlooking the river.

The original painting was a mural etched into the limestone cliff face, indicating its significance to the local Native American tribes. The imagery of the Piasa is believed to represent a spirit creature, which, according to some tribal stories, was both feared and revered, embodying the dual aspects of protector and destroyer.

The legends of the Piasa Bird vary among the Native American tribes in the Mississippi Valley. One popular narrative involves the creature terrorizing tribal villages, demanding sacrifices to quell its hunger. According to one version of the story, the Piasa would prey upon the tribe until a brave chief managed to kill the beast, thus saving his people. This tale positions the Piasa as a malevolent force, a common theme in the mythology surrounding mythical beasts.

Another interpretation suggests that the Piasa was once a great tribal warrior who was transformed into a monstrous bird as a punishment for overstepping human boundaries, possibly through acts of hubris or misuse of magic.

The image of the Piasa Bird is often used in ceremonial artifacts, tribal tattoos, and modern recreations, highlighting its lasting legacy.

Dark Spirits of Cherokee Mythology

Cherokee mythology, like that of many indigenous cultures, contains a rich tapestry of stories involving spirits and supernatural entities. Among these are tales of dark spirits—beings that embody the fears, challenges, and moral teachings of the Cherokee people.

Uktena: The Great Horned Serpent

One of the most formidable dark spirits in Cherokee mythology is Uktena, a giant serpent with horns, a jewel on its forehead, and scales that glitter like sparks of fire. According to legend, Uktena was once a man who transformed into a serpent, becoming a dangerous creature that could kill with a mere glance. The legends say that whoever could defeat Uktena and claim the jewel (Ulunsuti) would gain immense spiritual power.

Uktena represents both physical danger and spiritual corruption, symbolizing the perilous allure of forbidden knowledge and power. The stories of warriors seeking to confront Uktena are tales of bravery, but they also carry warnings about the destructive pursuit of power and the importance of humility and respect for the natural world.

Spearfinger: The Shape-shifting Witch

Another chilling figure in Cherokee lore is Spearfinger, a witch known for her sharp, obsidian finger which she used to cut out the livers of her victims. Spearfinger could disguise herself as a family member or a harmless old woman, using her powers of deception to trick her victims. Her ability to shape-shift speaks to the themes of trust and betrayal within the community.

Spearfinger's story is often told to children as a lesson in obedience and caution, teaching them to be wary of strangers and to stick to the paths known to be safe. This story also emphasizes the community's role in protecting its members from external threats, highlighting values of vigilance and collective responsibility.

The Raven Mocker: The Stealer of Souls

Perhaps the most feared of all Cherokee dark spirits is the Raven Mocker, an evil witch who can take the form of a raven. Raven Mockers are known to prey on the sick and dying, stealing their hearts and adding to their own lives the years their victims would have lived. The terror of the Raven Mocker lies not only in its actions but in its stealth, as it attacks at night and is almost impossible to catch.

The fear of the Raven Mocker reinforces the Cherokee's respect for the sick and elderly, emphasizing the need to protect the most vulnerable members of the community. It also underscores the deep Cherokee belief in the sanctity of the soul and the moral imperative to live a righteous life.

Afterword

The exploration of dark creatures across various cultures and religious traditions serves as more than a mere catalog of myths and folklore. It is a reflection of humanity's deepest fears, greatest challenges, and our enduring search for meaning within the chaos of existence.

Regardless of geographical and cultural divides, there is a common thread that connects these stories: the presence of demonic creatures as essential components of our spiritual and moral universes. They challenge heroes, frighten communities, and, perhaps most importantly, force individuals to confront their inner darkness.

Thank you for joining me on this fascinating exploration.

With warm regards,

Oscar Larsen

Printed in Great Britain
by Amazon